C000314922

maths match for the Un[illegible]lans

Pupil Book

6

Writing team Paul Broadbent
Len Frobisher
Jeanette Mumford
Allison Toogood

Harcourt Education Ltd
Halley Court, Jordan Hill, Oxford, OX2 8EJ

www.myprimary.co.uk
Help and support, plus the widest range of educational solutions.

© Harcourt Education Ltd 2004

This book is copyright and reproduction of the whole or part
without the publisher's written permission is prohibited.

First published 2004

08 07 06 05 04
10, 9, 8, 7, 6, 5, 4, 3, 2, 1

ISBN 0 433 09638 1

Illustrated by Mark Ruffle

Typesetting and layout by Artistix, Thame, Oxon

Printed and bound by Scotprint, Haddington, East Lothian

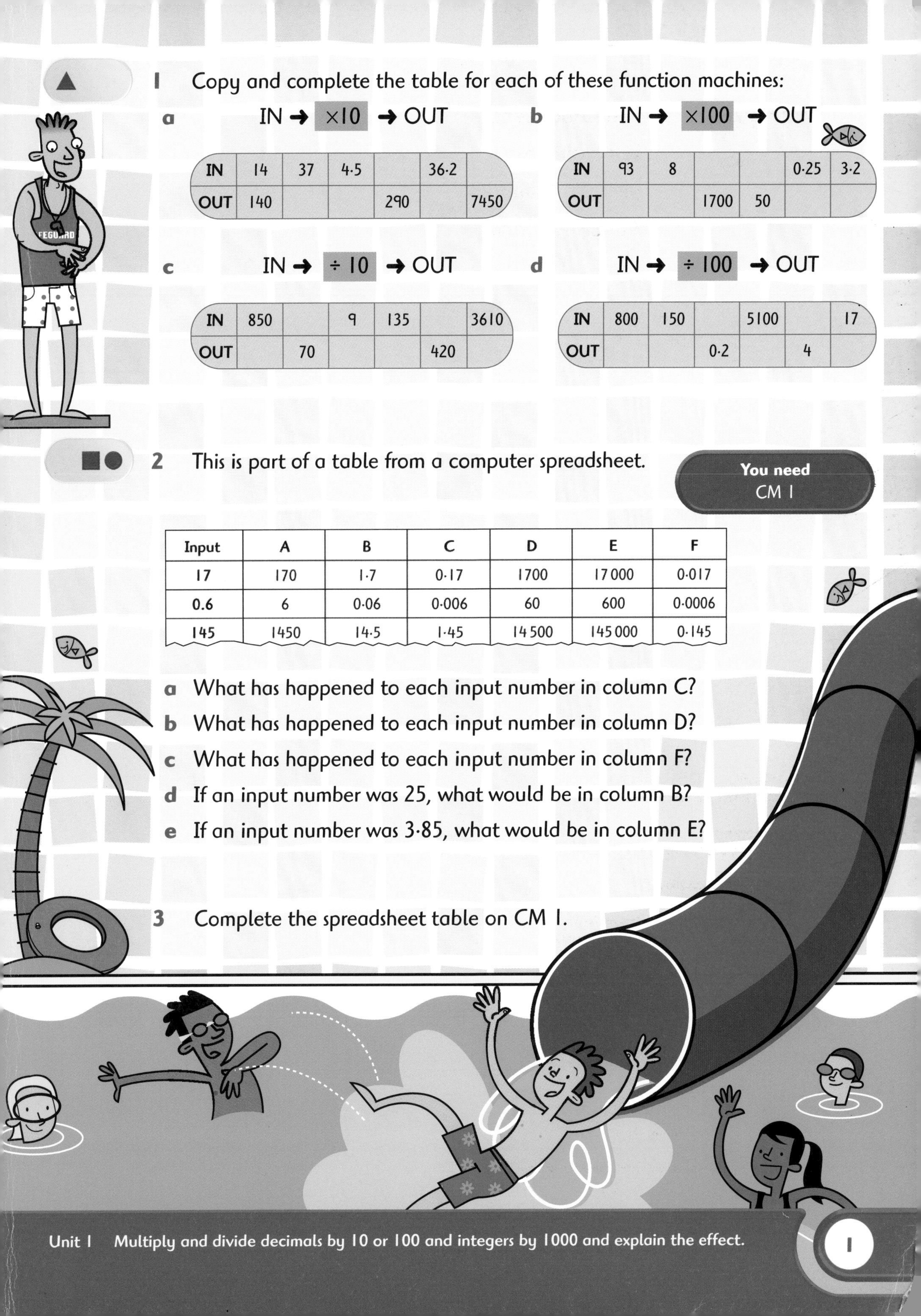

1 Copy and complete the table for each of these function machines:

a IN → ×10 → OUT

IN	14	37	4·5		36·2	
OUT	140			290		7450

b IN → ×100 → OUT

IN	93	8			0·25	3·2
OUT			1700	50		

c IN → ÷ 10 → OUT

IN	850		9	135		3610
OUT		70			420	

d IN → ÷ 100 → OUT

IN	800	150		5100		17
OUT			0·2		4	

2 This is part of a table from a computer spreadsheet.

You need
CM 1

Input	A	B	C	D	E	F
17	170	1·7	0·17	1700	17 000	0·017
0.6	6	0·06	0·006	60	600	0·0006
145	1450	14·5	1·45	14 500	145 000	0·145

a What has happened to each input number in column C?
b What has happened to each input number in column D?
c What has happened to each input number in column F?
d If an input number was 25, what would be in column B?
e If an input number was 3·85, what would be in column E?

3 Complete the spreadsheet table on CM 1.

1 This is a 'super-square':

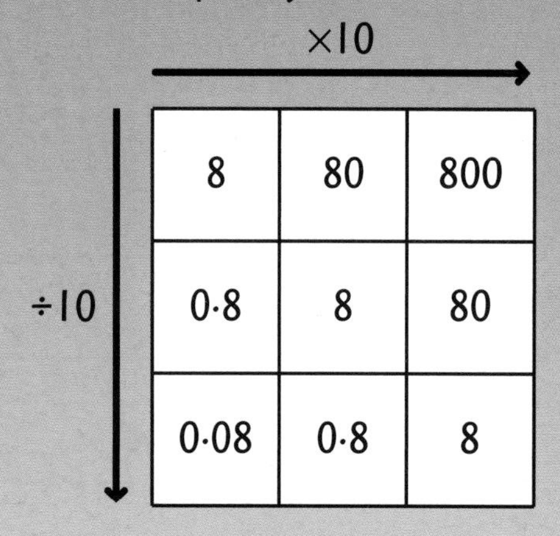

8	80	800
0·8	8	80
0·08	0·8	8

You need
CM 2

a Complete the super-squares on CM 2.

b Use the three blank squares at the bottom of CM 2 to create your own super-squares.

2 Play **Target Numbers.**

You need
1–9 digit cards

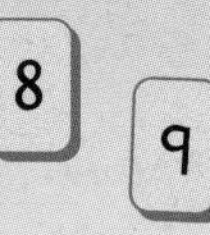

- Shuffle the cards and lay out six of them so they are arranged as two numbers, like this:

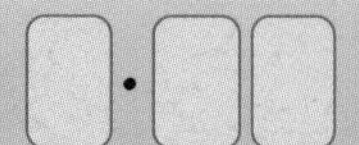
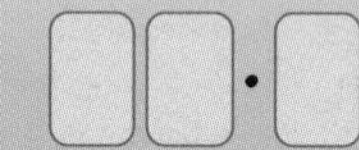

- Use any of these operations to change each of your numbers:

×10 ÷10 ×100 ÷100

- Add your new numbers together. Try to make the total as near as possible to one of these targets:

100 15 450 2

1 The table shows the approximate masses of balls used in different sports. Use the inverse operation to check your answers to these questions.

Sport	Mass of ball in grams
table tennis	2·5 g
golf	45 g
tennis	60 g
cricket	150 g
rugby	400 g
football	450 g
basketball	600 g
ten-pin bowling	7000 g

a How many golf balls will balance a football?

b What fraction of the mass of a basketball is a tennis ball?

c What is the mass in kilograms of 4 ten-pin bowls?

d How many cricket balls have the same mass as 3 basketballs?

e Table tennis balls come in sets of 10. How many sets of 10 table tennis balls have the same mass as a rugby ball?

f Which are heavier: 3 rugby balls and 2 tennis balls or 2 footballs and 9 golf balls?

2 Copy and complete each multiplication. Find and complete its matching division.

	Multiplication	Division
a	300 × ◯ = 1500	◯ ÷ 50 = 30
b	◯ × 50 = 1500	◯ ÷ 5 = 300
c	30 × ◯ = 150	◯ ÷ 5 = 3
d	◯ × 5 = 15	◯ ÷ 500 = 3
e	3 × ◯ = 150	◯ ÷ 5 = 0·3
f	◯ × 500 = 1500	◯ ÷ 5 = 30
g	0·3 × ◯ = 1·5	◯ ÷ 50 = 3

3 The two squares in each diagram contain the same number. Find two different ways to complete each diagram.

a 60 —×□→ ◯ —÷□→ ◯

b ◯ —×□→ 60 —÷□→ ◯

c ◯ —×□→ ◯ —÷□→ 60

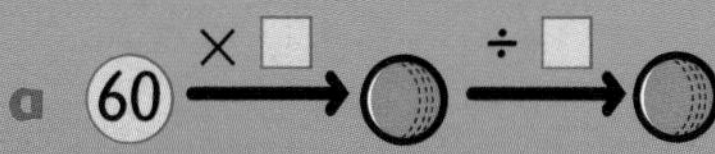

d ◯ —÷□→ ◯ —×□→ 2·5

e ◯ —÷□→ 2·5 —×□→ ◯

f 2·5 —÷□→ ◯ —×□→ ◯

1a The multiplex cinema has 14 screens with 150 seats in each. How many seats are there altogether?

b Popcorn costs £1·80. Every child in a group of 35 buys popcorn. What is the total cost?

c A film that lasts 75 minutes is shown 8 times every day. How many hours is the film shown each day?

d A youth group sends 25 minibuses to the cinema. Each minibus has 16 passengers. How many are in the minibuses altogether?

e The cinema has 25 identical parking areas. When they are all full there are 600 cars altogether. How many cars are in each parking area?

f The price of a cinema ticket is £6·50 for an adult and £3·40 for a child. At a showing of the film 'Aliens in Space' there are 35 adults and 45 children. How much money have they paid altogether?

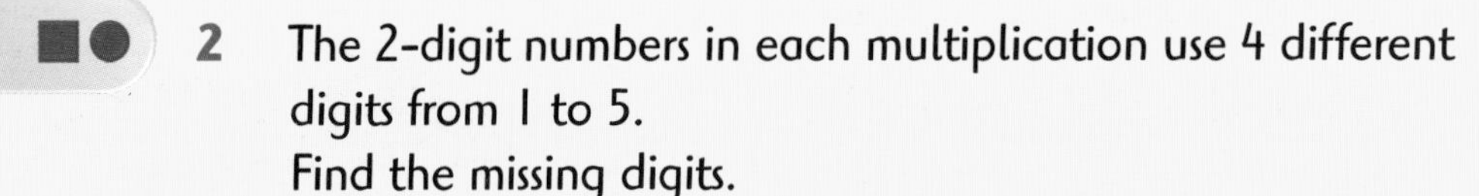

2 The 2-digit numbers in each multiplication use 4 different digits from 1 to 5.
Find the missing digits.

a [3][ ] × [1][ ] = 420 **b** [2][ ] × [5][ ] = 1113

c [4][ ] × [3][ ] = 1440 **d** [4][ ] × [2][ ] = 1075

3a What is the largest product that can be made using the digits 2, 3, 4 and 5?

b What is the smallest product that can be made using the digits 2, 3, 4 and 5?

1 The till in the shop *Games Station* is not working. The manager makes 'ready-reckoners' for the staff for two games that cost £23 and £34 each. Copy and complete the ready-reckoners.

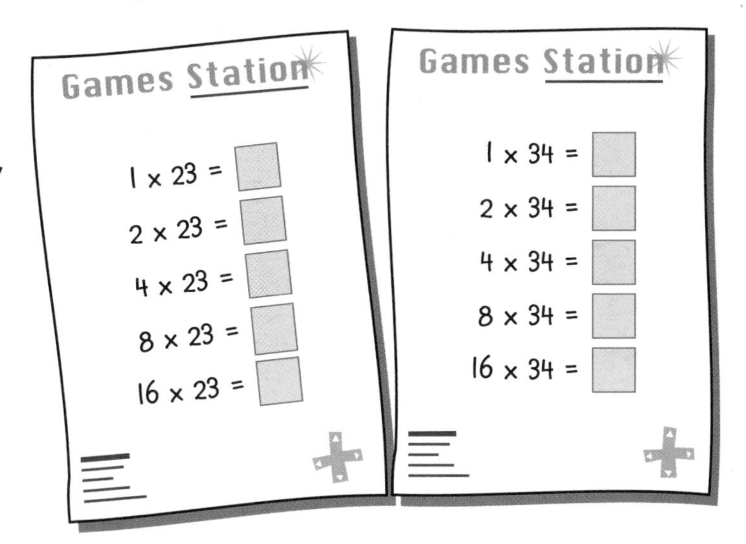

2 Use your ready-reckoners from question 1 to find:

a $6 \times £23$

b $5 \times £34$

c $7 \times £23$

d $9 \times £34$

e $12 \times £23$

f $14 \times £34$.

Show your working.

3 Use the two ready-reckoners together to find the total cost of:

a two games at £23 and one at £34

b one game at £23 and three at £34

c four games at £23 and two at £34

d five games at £23 and six at £34.

4a Show three different ways to find the cost of 18 games at £23 each using the ready-reckoner.

b Show two different ways of finding the cost of 18 games at £23 each that do <u>not</u> use the ready-reckoner.

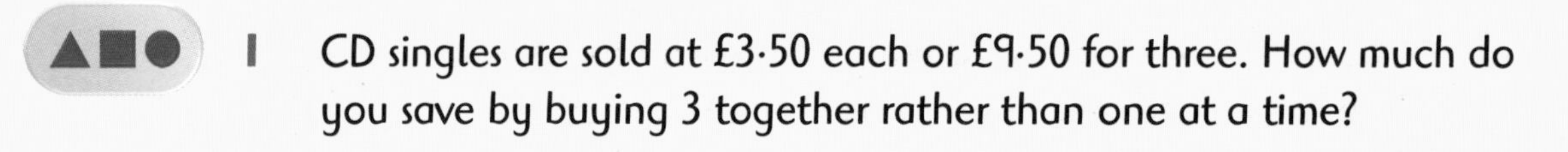

1 CD singles are sold at £3·50 each or £9·50 for three. How much do you save by buying 3 together rather than one at a time?

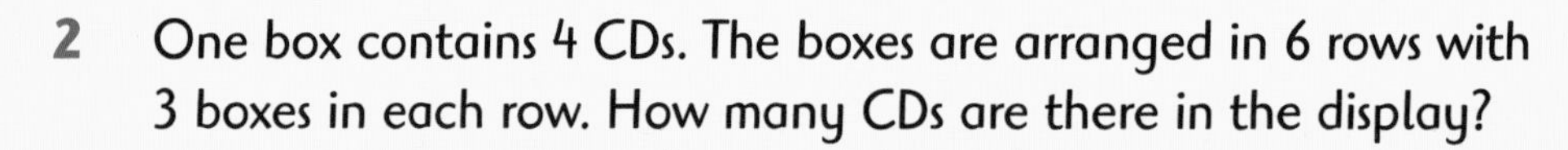

2 One box contains 4 CDs. The boxes are arranged in 6 rows with 3 boxes in each row. How many CDs are there in the display?

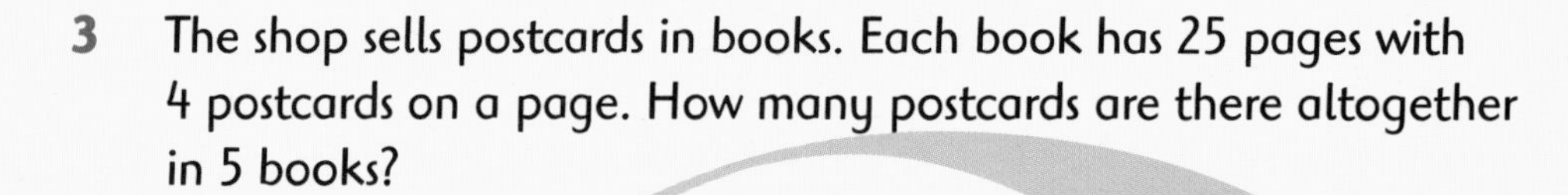

3 The shop sells postcards in books. Each book has 25 pages with 4 postcards on a page. How many postcards are there altogether in 5 books?

4 The shop receives a delivery of 40 CD racks. It already has 55 in stock. The CD racks are displayed in groups of 8. How many groups can be made? How many racks are left over?

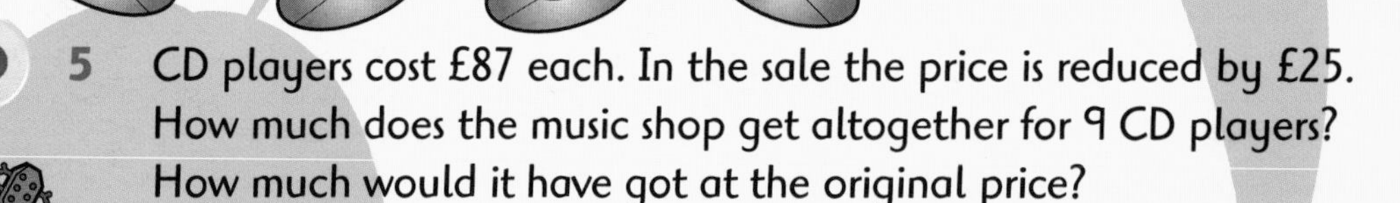

5 CD players cost £87 each. In the sale the price is reduced by £25. How much does the music shop get altogether for 9 CD players? How much would it have got at the original price?

6 Two deliveries of 35 boxes of headphones are made. Each box contains 6 headphones. How many headphones are delivered altogether?

7 It costs £39 to make a guitar. Eight guitars are sold at £89·50 each. What is the total profit made on the 8 guitars?

8 The shop sells 25 different posters. It has 64 boxes of each design, with 6 posters in each box. How many posters are for sale altogether?

9 The shop has 20 copies of each of 15 different jazz CDs at £12·98 each and 10 copies of each of 12 different classical CDs at £14·50 each. It sells $\frac{2}{3}$ of the jazz CDs and $\frac{3}{4}$ of the classical CDs at the full price. The rest are reduced by 50% in the sale.

a How many CDs are for sale altogether?

b How many CDs have been sold altogether? How many are in the sale?

c How much money has the shop taken for the CDs it has sold?

d What is the reduced price of:
- a jazz CD?
- a classical CD?

e How much money would the shop take by selling all the reduced CDs?

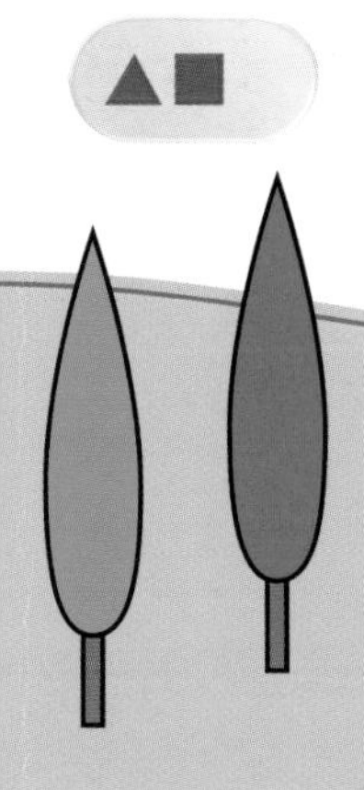

1 In a schools cross-country relay race each team has 8 runners. Each runner runs once round the course. The course is 683 metres long. How long is the race?

2 Winston School team trains by running 7 times around the school field. The distance around the school field is 179 metres. How far does each team member run?

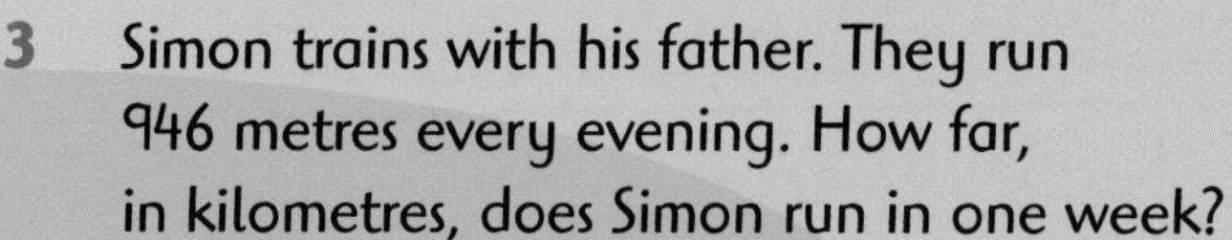

3 Simon trains with his father. They run 946 metres every evening. How far, in kilometres, does Simon run in one week?

4 Pete is keen on cyclo-cross. He cycles 37 kilometres 14 times a month. How many kilometres does he cycle in a month?

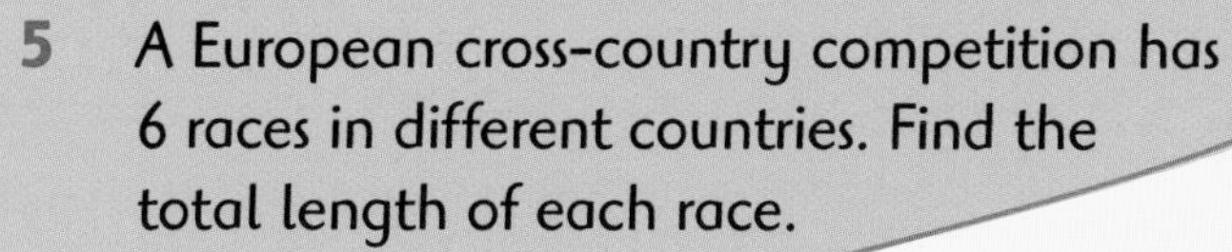

5 A European cross-country competition has 6 races in different countries. Find the total length of each race.

Country	Length of course	Number of laps of the course
Belgium	1·73 km	4
Spain	1·44 km	5
England	2·13 km	3
Scotland	1·86 km	4
Portugal	1·37 km	6
France	2·06 km	3

6a Use the digits 1 to 9 to complete these two multiplications:

☐☐ × ☐☐   ☐☐☐ × ☐☐

Find the sum of the your two products.

b Investigate making the sum of the two products as near as possible to 10 000.

1 For her birthday Alice received a pack of 450 stamps and a stamp album. Each page has space for 16 stamps. How many pages will have stamps on them?

2 Henry has a collection of 397 pin badges. He keeps them in boxes with 25 in a box.

a How many full boxes does he have?

b How many more badges does he need to fill another box?

3 Rose collects animal cards. She puts a rubber band around each group of 30 cards. Altogether she has 562 cards.

a How many groups of 30 does she have?

b How many cards are left over?

4 Class 6T collect 5p coins for charity. Between them 22 children collect 425 coins. What is the average number of coins per child? Round your answer to the nearest whole number.

5 Round the answer to each division up or down to the nearest whole number.

a $276 \div 35$ b $517 \div 26$ c $491 \div 43$ d $738 \div 29$

6 Each number in the table is rounded up and down after a division. Find the missing divisors.

Number	Divisor	Answer rounded up	Answer rounded down
111		14	13
222		19	18
333		20	19
444		20	19
555		19	18

7 The answer to a division is 24 r 18.

a Find five different divisions that have this answer.

b Use a calculator to write the answer to each division as decimals rounded to the nearest hundredth and tenth, and as a whole number.

You need a calculator

You need
a calculator

1 The Cubs in the Rotley Group have 4 tents with 8 Cubs in each tent.
How many Cubs are there altogether?

2 There are 49 Scouts in the Rotley Group.
Each tent sleeps 5.

a How many full tents will there be?

b How many will sleep in the partly full tent?

3 There are 84 Brownies and Guides in the Bradton Group.
For raft-making there are 4 teams of 9, and the rest are in teams of 12. How many teams of 12 are there?

4 In the Bradton Group the ratio of Guides to Brownies is 3 to 1. How many of each are there?

5 The cost of an activity weekend is £12 for Brownies and Cubs, and £15 for Guides and Scouts. In total there are 67 Cubs, 58 Brownies, 82 Guides and 78 Scouts. How much do they pay altogether?

6 A team of 8 Rotley Cubs and Scouts challenges a team of 12 Bradton Guides and Brownies to a tug of war. The Rotley team weighs 362 kilograms and the Bradton team weighs 375 kilograms. What is the difference in the average weight per person between the two teams?

▲ **1a** Take 8 cubes. Group them into quarters.

You need
cubes

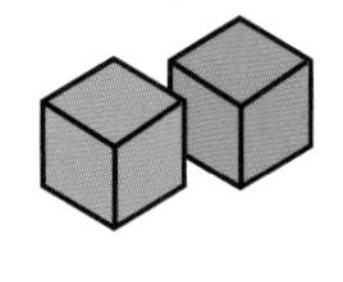
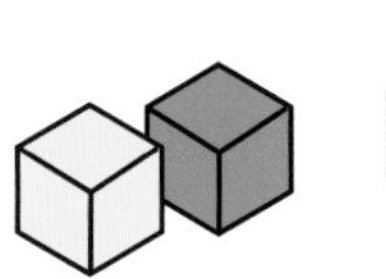
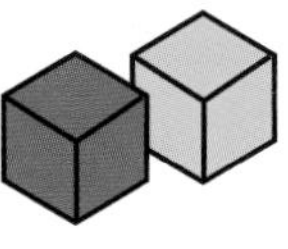

Do the same for: • 12 cubes • 16 cubes • 20 cubes

Write: • $\frac{1}{4} = \frac{\square}{8} = \frac{\square}{12} = \frac{\square}{16} = \frac{\square}{20}$ • $\frac{3}{4} = \frac{\square}{8} = \frac{\square}{12} = \frac{\square}{16} = \frac{\square}{20}$

b What do you notice about the denominators (bottom numbers)?

c What do you notice about the numerators (top numbers)?

d What if you had 24 cubes? Without using cubes, write one fraction equivalent to $\frac{1}{4}$ and one fraction equivalent to $\frac{3}{4}$. Explain how you did it.

▲■ **2** Ben knows straight away that $\frac{10}{39}$ cannot be equivalent to $\frac{1}{4}$ because 39 is not a multiple of 4.

a Sort the fractions on Ben's board into two sets:

- fractions that cannot be equivalent to $\frac{1}{4}$
- fractions that may be equivalent to $\frac{1}{4}$.

b Look at the fractions that may be equivalent to $\frac{1}{4}$. For each, decide if it is or is not, and explain why.

■● **3** Work with a partner.

You need
number cards 6–20

- Shuffle the cards and place them in a pile, face down. Take turns to pick up the top card.
- Write the set of fractions less than 1 with the number on your card as denominator. Change each one to its simplest equivalent fraction.
- Score a point for each fraction you have simplified.

● **4** Discuss the game in question 3.

You need
number cards 1–100

a Choose a set of 20 cards from number cards 1–100 to give you a high score.
Explain your choice and try it out.

b Are there ways you would like to change the game to improve it?
It must still include simplifying.
List your 3 best ideas with reasons for choosing them.

1a Change these fractions so that they all have the same denominator.

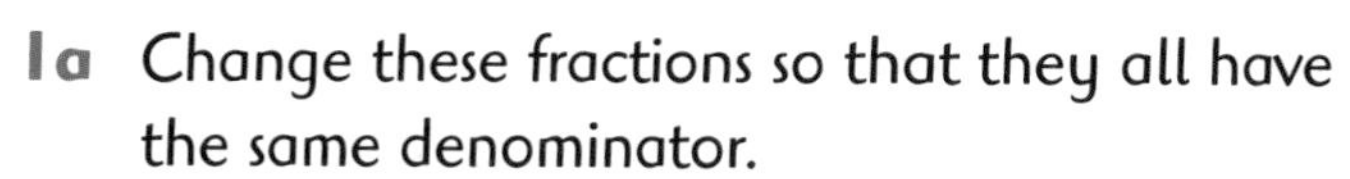

b Find them on a metre rule and write them in order, from smallest to largest.

c Write them in order as decimal fractions.

You need
a metre rule

Remember:
$1\text{ cm} = \frac{1}{100}\text{ m} = 0{\cdot}01\text{ m}$

2a Change these fractions so that they all have the same denominator.

Do not use the same denominator as in question **1a**.

b Draw a number line 10 cm long. Mark it in tenths and write on the fractions.

c Write one fraction that comes between $\frac{1}{2}$ and $\frac{7}{10}$.
Change it to a simpler fraction, if you can.

3 Work in a group.

a Make a set of 8 fractions. Include different fifths, tenths, quarters and hundredths.

Predict their order, from smallest to largest.

b Use a metre rule.

- Draw a number line 1 m long.
- Position your fractions accurately above the line and label them. Was your prediction correct?
- Write the equivalent decimal fractions below the line.

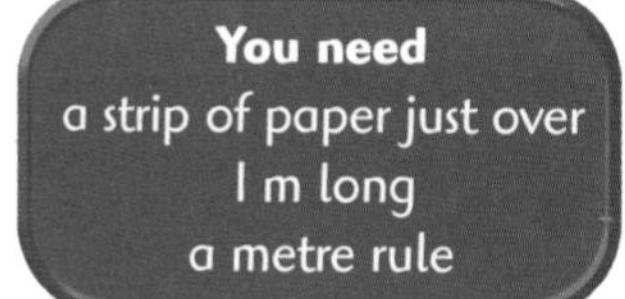

4 Draw another 1 m number line on the other side of the paper. Repeat question **3** but this time begin by making a set of 4 fractions. Then write down 4 decimal fractions so you have 8 numbers altogether. Don't forget to predict the order before you record them on the line.

5 Follow the instructions in questions **3** and **4**, but include eighths and twelfths too.

You need
a calculator

▲ **1** Find $\frac{1}{4}$ of: **1 m** **1 km** **1 l** **1 kg**

Write:

a 0·25 m = □ mm **b** 0·25 km = □ m

c 0·25 l = □ ml **d** 0·25 kg = □ g

Remember:
1 m = 1000 mm
1 km = 1000 m
1 l = 1000 ml
1 kg = 1000 g

▲■ **2a** Ryan puts 1 litre of petrol in his go-kart's fuel tank.

- He uses $\frac{1}{4}$ of it. How many millilitres does he have left?
- How many litres does he have left?
- What percentage of the petrol does he have left?

b He races for 10 laps round the track, a total of 2·5 km.

- How many metres is 10 laps?
- How many metres is 1 lap?
- How many kilometres is 1 lap?
- What percentage of the race is 1 lap?

c Ryan's helmet has a mass of 0·4 kg. Write its mass in grams.

■● **3** Go-karts have to be less than 1500 mm long and less than 800 mm wide.

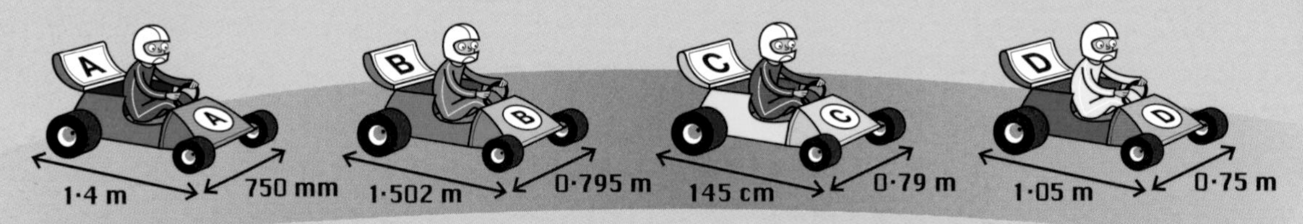

a Which of these go-karts are allowed to race? Explain your answer.

b What percentage of these go-karts are allowed to race?

c Change one dimension so that all the go-karts are allowed to race.

● **4** The fuel tank in each go-kart holds 2 litres of petrol when full.
The mechanic measures what is left in each tank.

a 1·5 l **b** 0·6 l **c** 1·14 l **d** 0·98 l

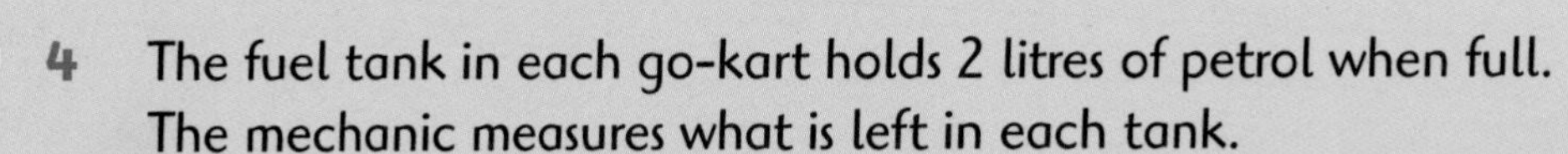

- How much fuel, in millilitres, has each kart used?
- What percentage of a full tank has each kart used?

e What if 1·75 l was left in one tank?
Find the percentage of the fuel that has been used.

1 Copy and complete the table of distances.

	100 m	200 m	400 m	800 m
5%			20 m	
10%				80 m
15%		30 m		
20%			80 m	
25%	25 m		100 m	

2 Some go-karts broke down before the end of their race. How far did they get?

a completed 15% of 220 m

b completed 20% of 480 m

c completed 80% of 800 m

d completed 55% of 1 km

3 Twenty go-karts started a race, but 30% did not finish.

a What percentage of the go-karts finished?

b How many go-karts finished?

c Make up a similar problem for your partner to answer.

4 Petrol costs 80p per litre at Fastfuel. Work out the prices at these petrol stations:

a 

b 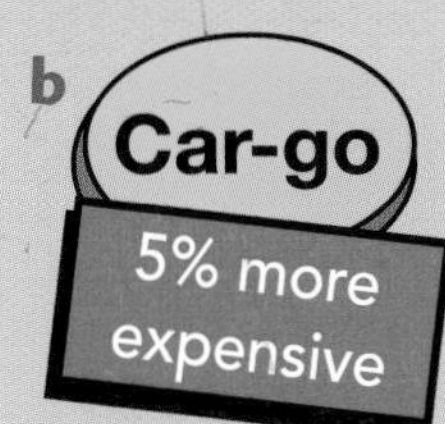

c 

d 

5a Fastfuel reduces its price by 10% to match Fill-up. A week later it increases the price by 10%. What is the price now?

b Explain why the increased price is not the same as the original price.

6 A survey asked where drivers buy their petrol. Look at the pie chart of the results.

a 15 buy at Fastfuel. What percentage is this?

b How many drivers took part in the survey?

c Find how many buy at the other petrol stations.

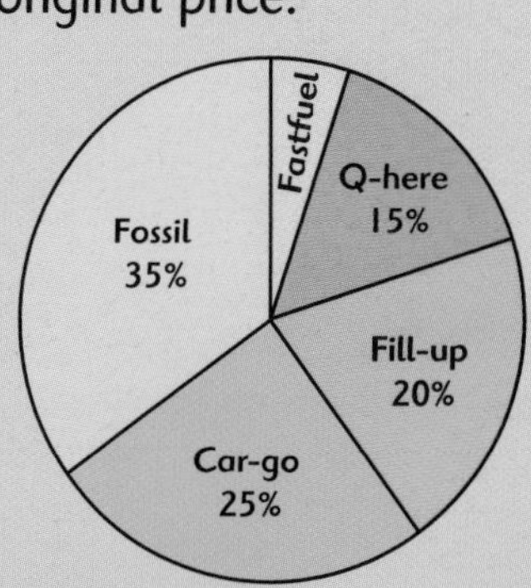

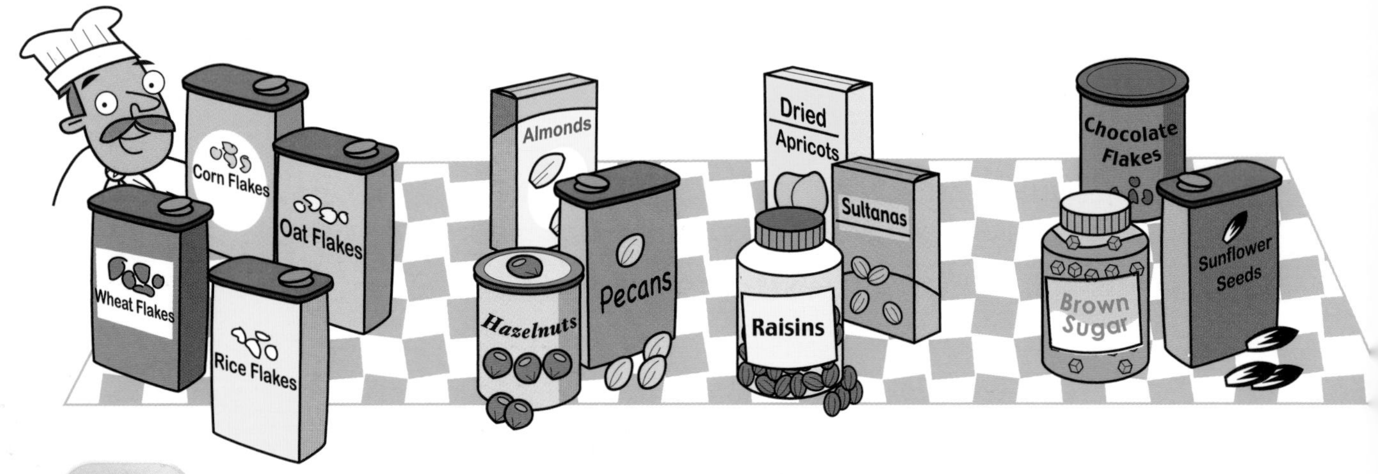

1 Use any of the ingredients from the kitchen to design a breakfast cereal for each of these 100 g boxes.

For each box:

- write the percentage of other ingredients
- list how many grams of each ingredient.

2 Chico the chef is experimenting with five new breakfast cereals.
He wants to make 100 g of each and has already decided on the proportion of one ingredient in each cereal.

a Recipe 1	**b** Recipe 2	**c** Recipe 3	**d** Recipe 4	**e** Recipe 5
Chocolate flakes 0·1	Sunflower seeds $\frac{1}{20}$	Sultanas 9%	Pecans 7·5%	Dried apricots $\frac{1}{8}$

Use ingredients from the kitchen to complete Chico's recipes.
For each recipe:

- choose other ingredients and write the proportions
- list how much of each ingredient in grams and in kilograms.

3 Chico's favourite cereal is a mixture of flakes with these proportions of special ingredients:

- dried apricots 0·05
- almonds 0·025
- brown sugar $\frac{1}{8}$
- raisins $\frac{1}{25}$.

a What percentage of flakes does he need to make this cereal?

b Explain how to make 200 g of this cereal from the ingredients in Chico's kitchen.

▲ **1** Chico has £10 to buy more ingredients.

a Round each price on his list to the nearest pound to see if he has enough money.

b Round each price on his list to the nearest 10p to estimate how much change he will get.

c Use a calculator to find the exact total cost.

d Chico has forgotten to put 1 kg of cherries on his list. They cost £1·21 for 500 g. Can he afford to buy them?

e Write the prices for 1 kg of each ingredient in order, from lowest to highest, including the cherries.

You need
a calculator

1kg of:

Wheat flakes	£0.72
Dried apricots	£2.48
Sultanas	£1.25
Jumbo oats	£0.59
Hazelnuts	£3.76

■● **2a** For each set of 3 scales on CM 3, choose a mass that lies between the 2 masses shown. Record it on the middle scale.

b Under each scale, record the mass
- to the nearest kilogram
- to the nearest tenth of a kilogram.

You need
CM 3
a calculator

3 Do the same for the measuring jugs on CM 3.
Round to the nearest litre and to the nearest tenth of a litre.

4 Chico used to measure ingredients using imperial units.

1 pint ≈ $\frac{3}{5}$ of a litre *1 pound (lb) ≈ $\frac{5}{11}$ of a kilogram*

a Put these amounts of milk in order, from smallest to largest:
0·85 l 1 pint 1000 ml $1\frac{1}{2}$ pints 500 ml $\frac{1}{2}$ pint

b Put these amounts of flour in order, from largest to smallest:
2 lb 2500 g 10 lb $\frac{1}{2}$ lb 0·75 kg $\frac{1}{3}$ kg

Round the amounts to the nearest tenth, then order them.

● **5** A more accurate fraction for converting pints to litres is $\frac{5}{9}$. Use it to convert the imperial amounts in question **4a** to the nearest hundredth of a litre.
Does the order change?

1 pint ≈ $\frac{5}{9}$ litre

▲

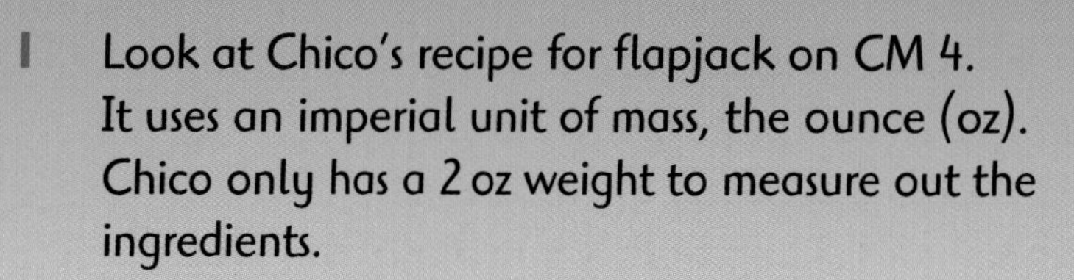

1 Look at Chico's recipe for flapjack on CM 4.
It uses an imperial unit of mass, the ounce (oz).
Chico only has a 2 oz weight to measure out the ingredients.
He uses it once to measure out the sugar.
He uses it twice to measure out the butter.

You need
CM 4

Copy and complete:

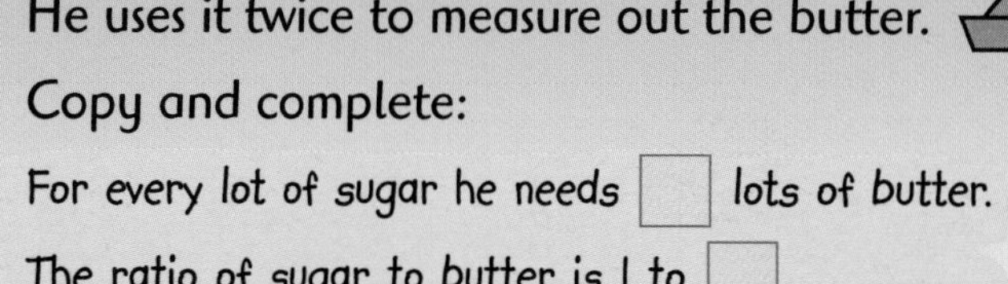

a For every lot of sugar he needs ☐ lots of butter.
The ratio of sugar to butter is 1 to ☐.

b For every lot of sugar he needs ☐ lots of oats.
The ratio of sugar to oats is ☐ to ☐.

▲■

2 The recipe for flapjack on CM 4 makes 12 pieces.
Chico needs to make 24 pieces.

You need
CM 4

a Write how much of each ingredient he needs.

b Draw pieces of flapjack on plates **A**, **B** and **C** on CM 4 to match these proportions:

- **A**: $\frac{1}{4}$ of 24 • **B**: $\frac{1}{3}$ of 24 • **C**: $\frac{1}{12}$ of 24.

What proportion of the 24 pieces is left for plate **D**?

c Decorate the pieces of flapjack with cherries in these ratios:

- Plate **A**: 1 piece with a cherry to 2 pieces without
- Plate **B**: 1 piece with a cherry to 3 pieces without
- Plate **C**: 1 piece with a cherry to 1 piece without
- Plate **D**: 3 pieces with a cherry to 5 pieces without.

d How many cherries did you need altogether?

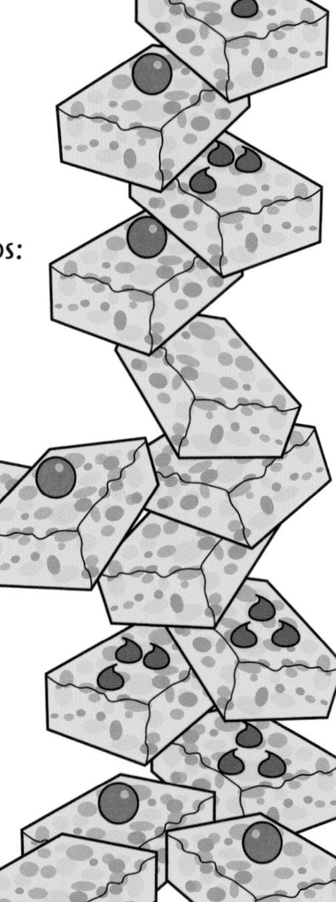

■

3 Decorate the remaining pieces of flapjack on CM 4 with chocolate chips.
Write the proportion of pieces with chocolate on each plate.

4 Investigate how much of each ingredient you would need to make one piece of flapjack for each child in a class of 30 children.

5 With metric measures, Chico's flapjack recipe makes 15 pieces. Instead of 8 oz of porridge oats, 4 oz of butter and 2 oz of sugar, the recipe uses 250 g of porridge oats, 125 g of butter and 60 g of sugar. Investigate how much of each ingredient you would need to make 100 pieces, like this:

You need a calculator

a Estimate to 1 decimal place what you need to multiply 15 by to make 100.

b Try it out on a calculator and improve your estimate if you can.

c Multiply the original quantity of each ingredient by your estimate to find how much you would need for 100 pieces (to the nearest 10 g).

6 Look at Chico's recipe for gingerbread on CM 5.

You need CM 5

a What is the total mass of all the ingredients?

b Complete the table showing the proportion of each ingredient as a fraction, a decimal and a percentage.

Find the simplest equivalent fraction.

Ingredient	Fraction	Decimal	Percentage
flour	$\frac{200}{500} = \frac{2}{5}$		
butter			
golden syrup			

7 Write four different equivalent ratios for each of these:

a 1 to 4 **b** 3 to 2 **c** 4 to 5 **d** 20 to 3

For example: 1 to 2 is equivalent to 2 to 4, 5 to 10, 25 to 50 and 500 to 1000.

8 For Chico's gingerbread recipe, work out the ratio of:

a flour to butter

b flour to golden syrup

c butter to golden syrup

d ginger and mixed spice to flour.

Try to write the simplest equivalent ratio.

9 Each slab of Chico's gingerbread makes 18 pieces. Find how much of each ingredient you would need to make one piece of gingerbread for each child in a class of 30 children.

You need a calculator

1a If this spinner was spun once, find the probability that it would land on:

You need
CM 6

A yellow
B red
C blue
D red or yellow
E yellow or blue
F red or blue
G green
H any of red, yellow or blue.

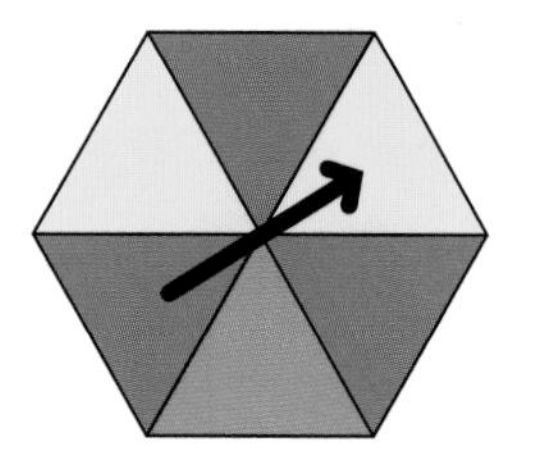

b Write the letters on the probability scale on CM 6.

2a On CM 6, colour the spinners to match each of these descriptions:

You need
CM 6
coloured pencils

Spinner	Probability
A	An even chance of landing on red.
B	The same chance of landing on red as on yellow.
C	Twice the chance of landing on blue as on red.
D	An even chance of landing on either red or yellow.
E	A 1 in 8 chance of landing on yellow, a 3 in 8 chance of landing on red and a 1 in 2 chance of landing on blue.

b Decide how to colour spinners F, G and H.
Write the probability for each colour below each spinner.

3 Work with a partner.

You need
interlocking triangles

a Use blue and red tiles. Build octahedra that, when rolled, have these probabilities:
- an equal chance of landing on a red or a blue face
- a $\frac{3}{8}$ chance of landing on a blue face.

b Use blue, red and green tiles. Build octahedra with:
- a 1 in 4 chance of landing on a green face
- an even chance of landing on a blue face and a $\frac{1}{8}$ chance of landing on a red face.

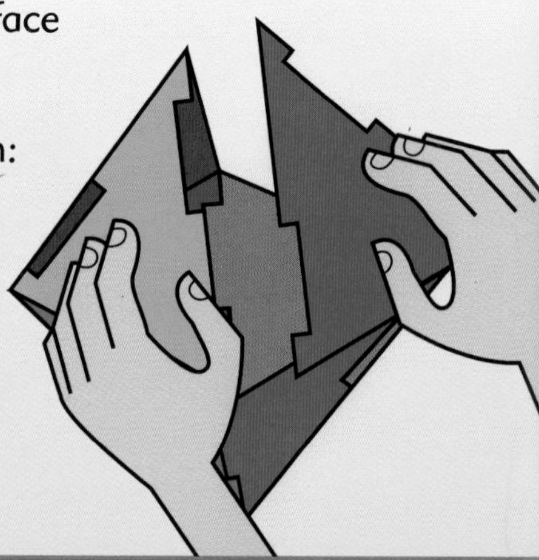

Unit 6a Use the language associated with probability to discuss events, including those with equally likely outcomes.

1 Ashni and Krishnan bought a new game.
They wrote down their scores for the first week.

You need
squared paper

33	2	25	14	20	23	39	28
26	24	32	9	22	14	21	31
23	12	27	28	16	18	5	10
38	23	26	40	19	22	31	26
34	25	22	8	17	20	24	29

a Copy and complete the frequency table.

b Which class interval had the highest frequency?

c Draw a bar chart to show the results.

Score	Tally	Frequency
1–5		
6–10		

2 Two weeks later the children recorded these scores.

a Draw a bar chart.

b Which class interval had the highest frequency?

c Compare the two bar charts for scores:
- between 1 and 10
- between 11 and 20
- between 21 and 30
- between 31 and 40.

Write about what you notice.

Score	Frequency
1–5	0
6–10	1
11–15	2
16–20	5
21–20	9
26–30	12
31–35	7
36–40	4

3 Work with a partner.
- Take turns to roll all four dice and record the total. Do this 20 times each.
- Decide together on the class intervals and each make a frequency table of your results.
- Each draw a bar chart to show your own results.
- Compare bar charts and decide who had the higher scores. Justify your answer.

You need
four 7–12 dice

1 The graph shows how far some children kicked a ball during practice.

a Find the range and the mode of the length of the kicks.

b Write the length of every kick in order, from shortest to longest. Find the median distance.

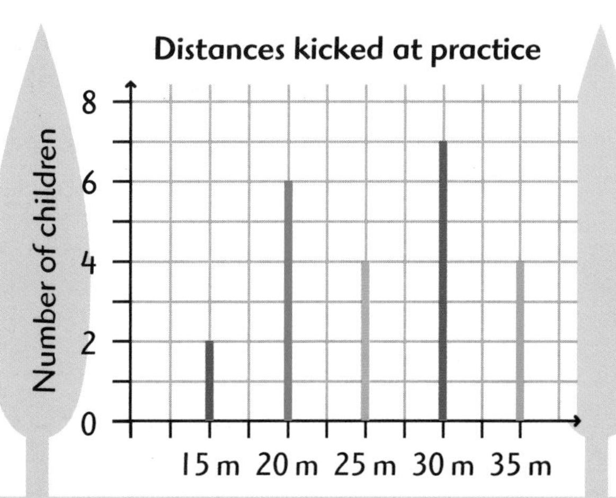

2 Teams of five children took part in a basketball shoot-out.

Team	Scores
Red	1 8 3 5 3
Green	7 6 2 3 7
Blue	4 4 5 4 6
White	3 5 6 6 4

a For each team:

- Find the range and mode of the scores.
- Write the scores in order, from smallest to largest, and find the median score.
- Work out the mean score.
- Record your results in a table.

Team	Range	Mode	Median	Mean
Red				
Green				
Blue				
White				

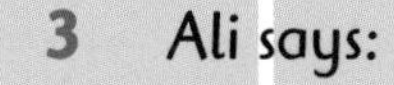

b Which team won? Justify your answer.

3 Ali says:

In each training session I do an average of 20 press-ups.

Number of press-ups				
M	T	W	Th	F
21	18	19	17	20
20	19	16	15	22
16	20	18	18	19
21	23	20	20	18

a Find the mean from his press-ups record over four weeks.

b Decide whether his claim is true.

1a Use the graph to convert these temperatures to °F:

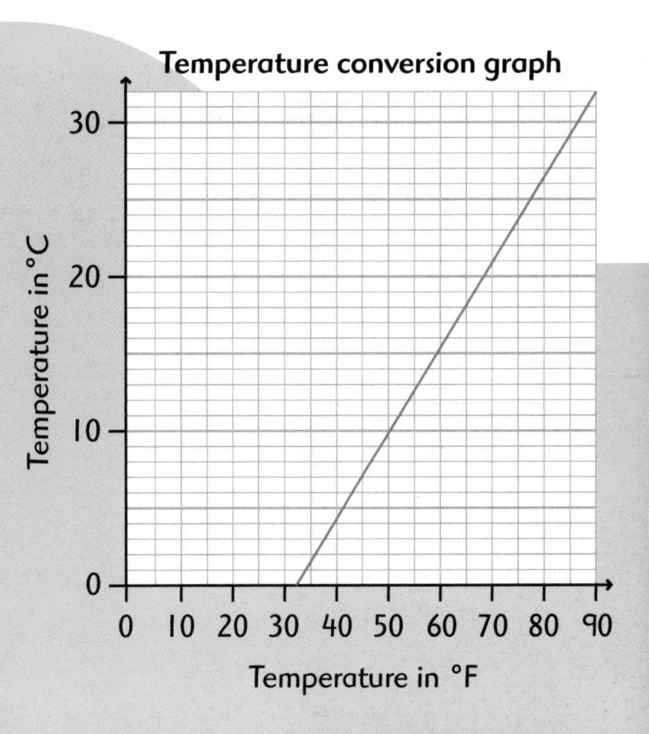

b Use the graph to convert these temperatures to °C:

80°F 35°F 60°F 40°F 55°F

2a Copy and complete the approximate conversion table.

Litres	Pints
1	1·75
2	
3	
4	
5	

You need squared paper

b Use the table to draw a conversion graph.

c Find how many pints there are in:

- 4·5 l
- 3·8 l
- 2·4 l
- 400 ml.

d Find how many litres there are in:

- 2·5 pints
- 5·5 pints
- 3·75 pints
- $\frac{1}{2}$ pint.

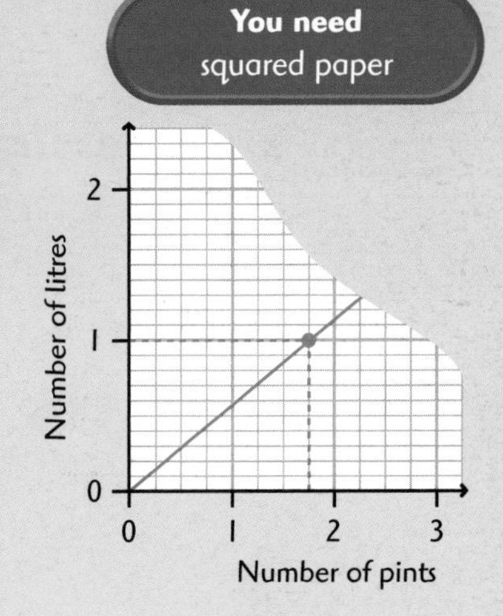

3 The graph shows the cost of hiring a bike. It costs £5 per day plus a fixed charge of £20.

a Find the cost of hiring a bike for:

- 4 days
- 8 days.

b You pay £50. For how many days have you hired a bike?

c Draw a graph to show the cost of renting a speedboat with a fixed charge of £8 plus £2 per hour.

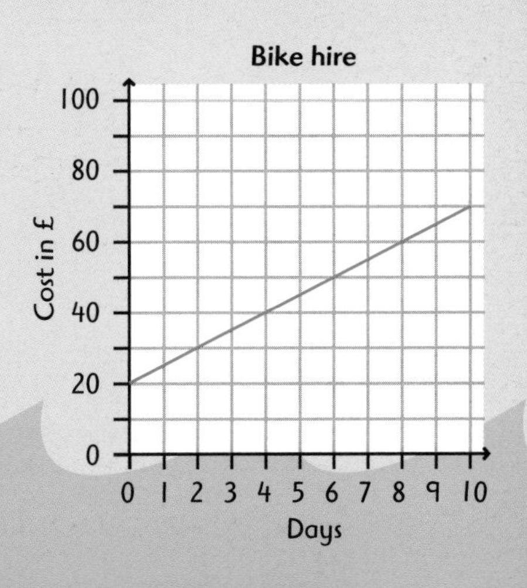

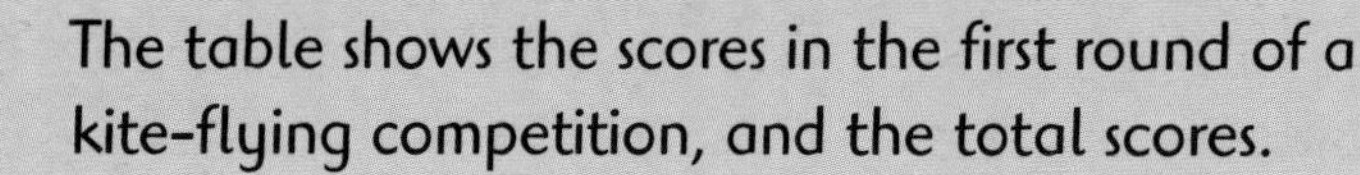

1 The table shows the scores in the first round of a kite-flying competition, and the total scores.

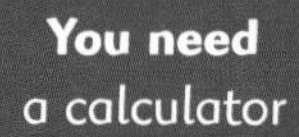

Name	1st round score (out of 1000)	2nd round score (out of 1000)	Total score (out of 2000)
Damien	683		1305
Sanjeev	714		1288
Zoe	579		1312
Jemma	462		1205
Meena	863		1314

a Find each person's scores in the second round.

b Check using a calculator and the inverse operation.

2 Press these keys on your calculator. Record the final display.

a 2 6 7 + 5 9 4 =

b 6 8 3 + 7 4 C 7 6 0 =

c 9 5 + 6 5 1 AC 7 7 5 – 6 1 8 =

d From parts **b** and **c**, explain the effect of the C and AC keys.

3 For each calculation below, estimate whether the answer will be:

- less than 500
- equal to 500
- more than 500.

You need
a calculator

Then use a calculator to find the exact answer.

a $8{\cdot}3 \times 7{\cdot}2 \times 6{\cdot}1$

b $(23{\cdot}2 \times 12) + 221{\cdot}6$

c $987{\cdot}6 - (5{\cdot}6 \times 78{\cdot}9)$

d $876 \div (0{\cdot}54 + 3{\cdot}21)$

4a Use the digits 1 to 9 to complete this calculation:

$\square\square{\cdot}\square\square \div (\square{\cdot}\square + \square{\cdot}\square\square)$

Use a calculator to find the answer.

b Investigate making an answer as near to 1 as possible.

You need a calculator

1 Four children each throw two darts. The key shows what they must multiply each dart score by to find the total score. Write the four scores in order, largest first.

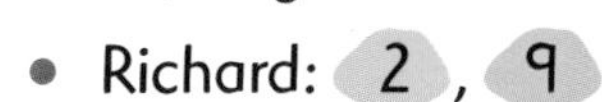

- Richard: 2, 9
- Sally: 10, 1
- Thomas: 5, 8
- Una: 4, 7

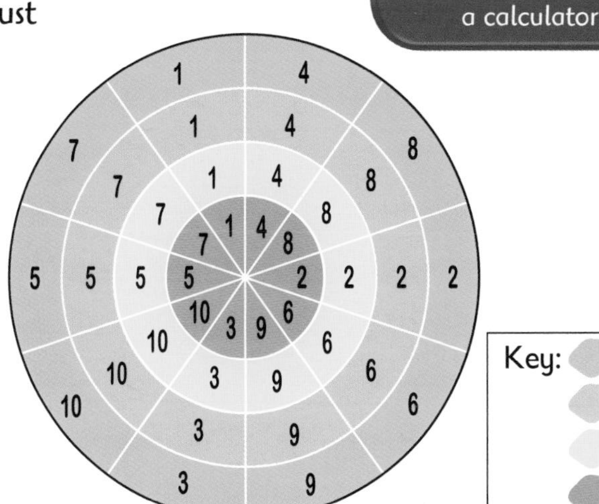

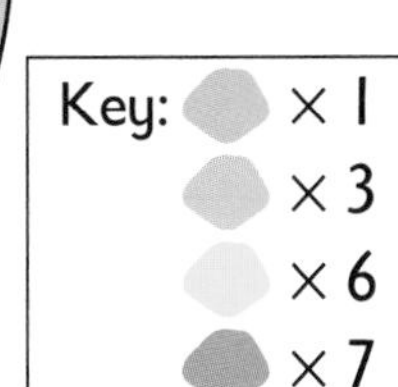

2 Use brackets to write how you can score each of these totals with two darts that land on the colours shown.

a 31: ? and ? b 36: ? and ? c 90: ? and ?

For each calculation, draw the calculator keys you would press to find the total score.

3 With three darts, find a total score between:

a 60 and 90 b 90 and 120.

Write the colour and the number for each dart.

Each dart must score on a different colour.

4 Enter each key sequence below and record the final display.

a [3] [2] [2] [÷] [7] [=] [M+] [6] [3] [8] [−] [2] [7] [5] [=] [×] [MR] [=]

b [5] [6] [×] [3] [7] [=] [M+] [2] [2] [×] [1] [4] [=] [M−] [MR] [=]

Write the calculation for each sequence of key presses.

5 Test what Sophie says using some sets of 2-digit and 3-digit consecutive numbers.
Is what Sophie says always true?
Explain why.

The product of any 3 consecutive integers is divisible by 6.

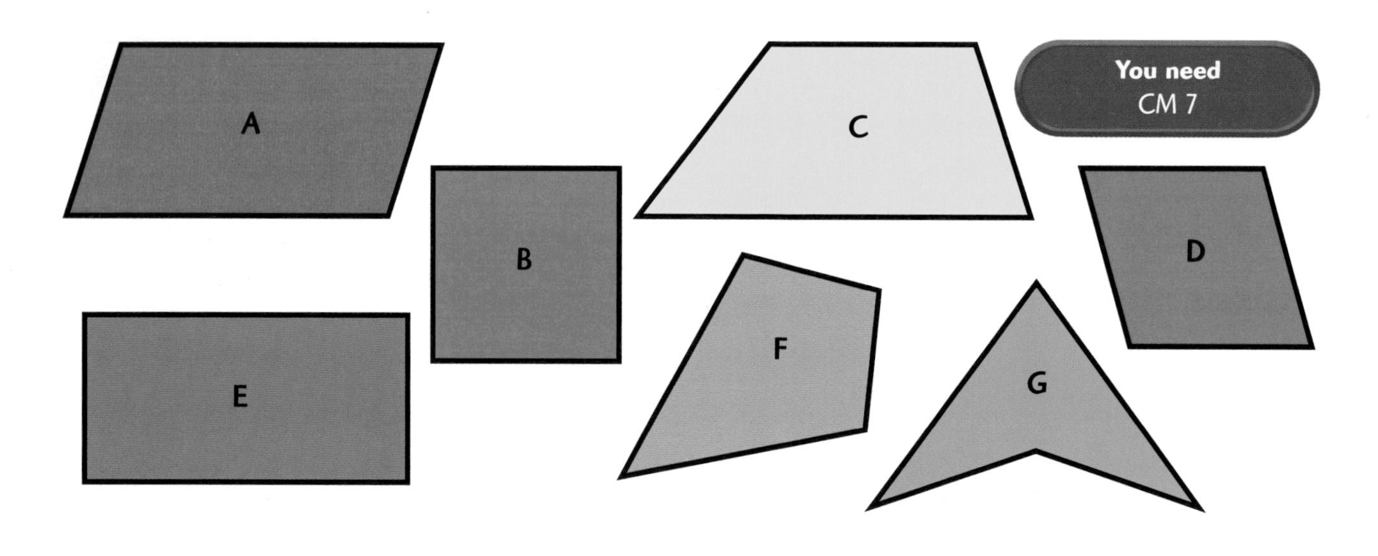

1a Name each of the quadrilaterals shown above.

b Sort the quadrilaterals onto the Carroll diagram on CM 7.
Sketch the shapes or write the shape letters in the correct positions.

2 Answer these questions with 'yes' or 'no'.

a *Are all rectangles parallelograms?*

b *Are all rhombuses parallelograms?*

c *Are all rhombuses squares?*

d *Are all trapeziums parallelograms?*

e *Are all kites parallelograms?*

f *Are all squares rectangles?*

3 For each part of question 2 where you gave the answer 'no', explain the reason for your decision.

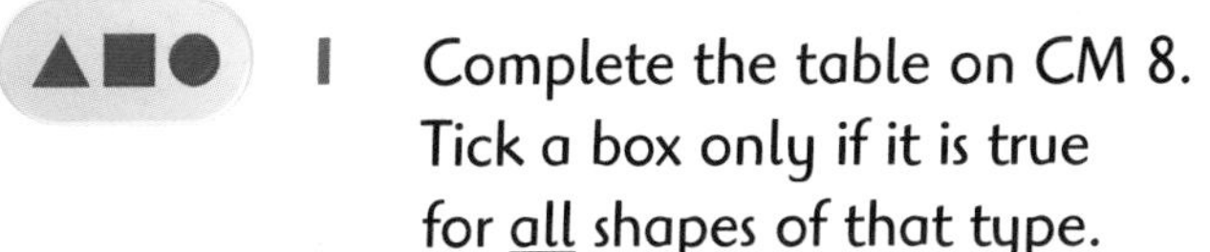

1 Complete the table on CM 8. Tick a box only if it is true for <u>all</u> shapes of that type.

You need
CM 8

	quadrilateral	parallelogram	rhombus	rectangle	square	kite	arrowhead	trapezium
has four sides	✓	✓	✓	✓	✓	✓	✓	✓
all sides same length								
opposite sides same length								
adjacent sides same length								
both pairs of opposite sides parallel								
at least one pair of opposite sides parallel								
at least one right angle								

2

How are rhombuses like squares?

How are parallelograms like rhombuses?

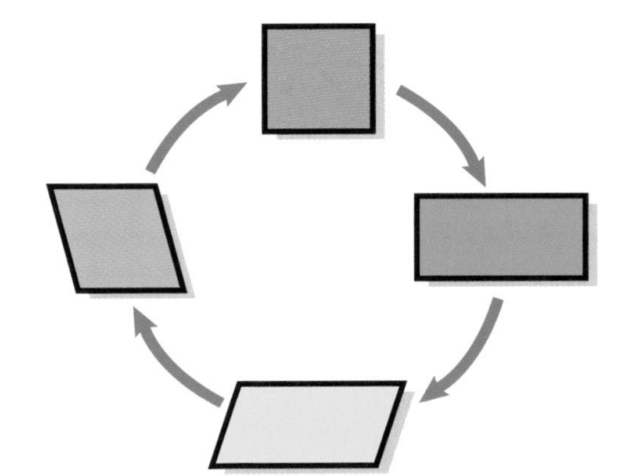

How are squares like rectangles?

How are rectangles like parallelograms?

a Write a description of the ways in which the shapes are similar.

b Now write the ways in which they are different.

1a Draw each shape on 1 cm squared paper and find its perimeter.

You need
1 cm squared paper

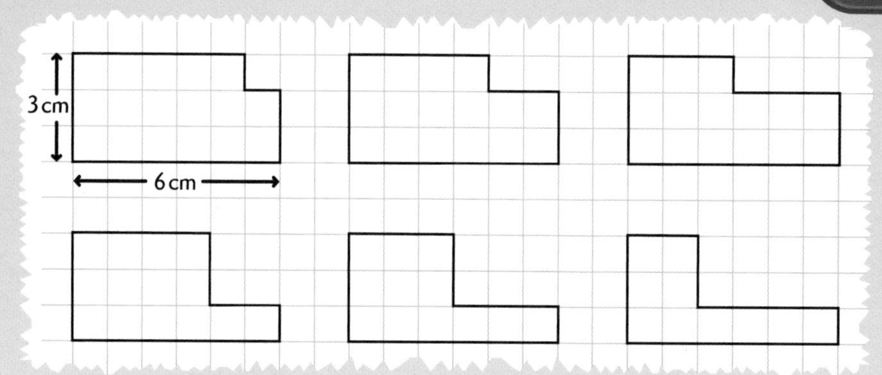

b What if the length of each side was doubled?

2 Find the perimeter of each shape.

a

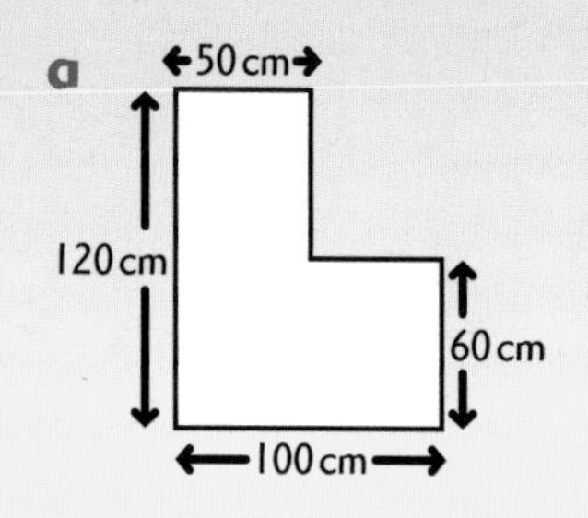

b

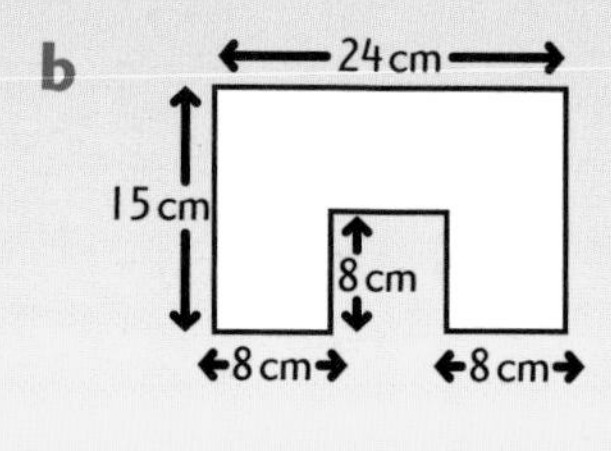

c

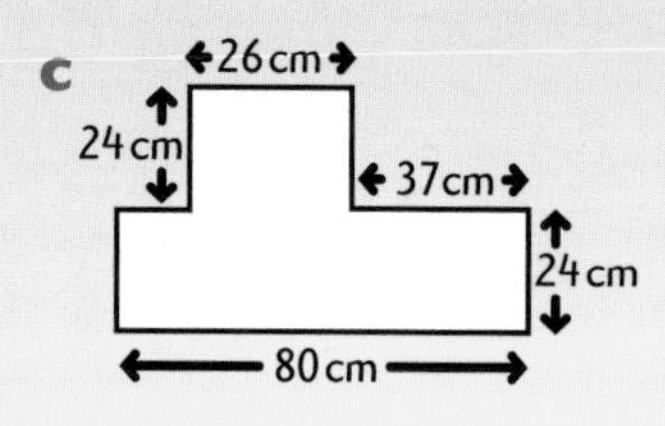

d

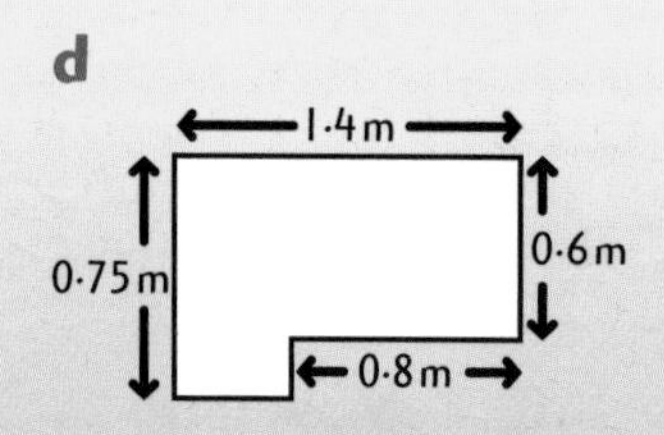

e

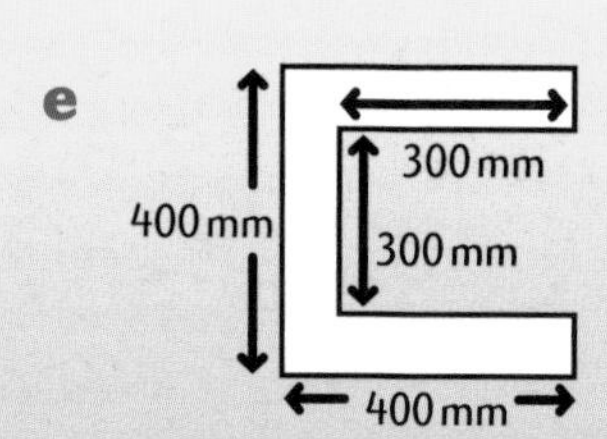

f

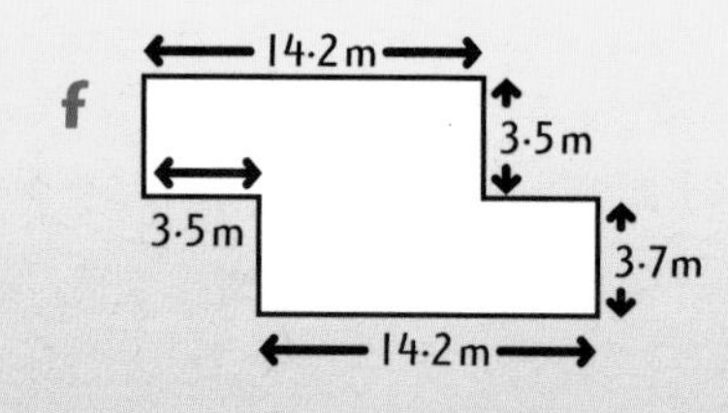

3a Find the perimeter of each shape in centimetres.

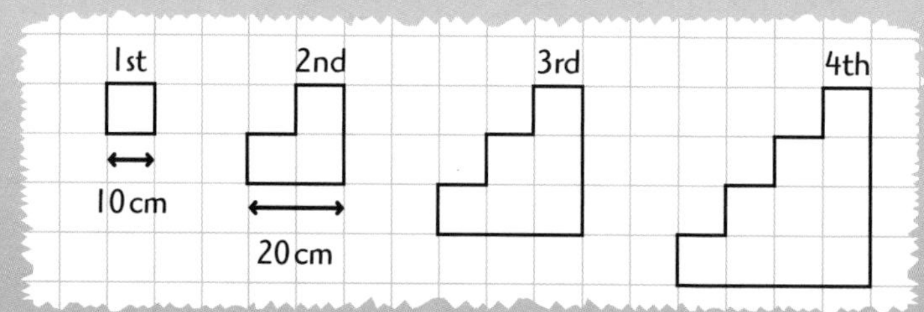

b Calculate the perimeter of the next two shapes in the sequence.

Record your answers in a table.

Shape	1st	2nd	3rd	4th	5th	6th
Perimeter (cm)						

c Predict and test for the perimeter of: • the 10th shape • the *n*th shape.

1 Each of these shapes is an edge-to-edge arrangement of square tiles. Find the perimeter and area of each shape.

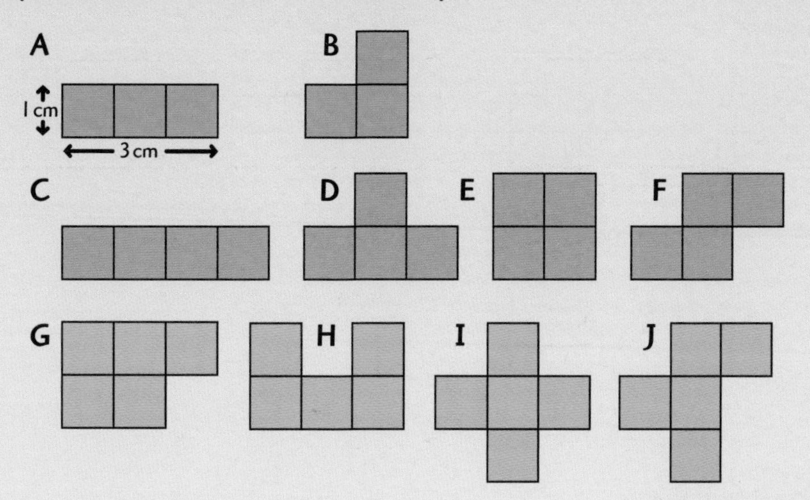

2 Shapes A, B and C are drawn on 1 cm squared paper. They are made by joining a blue and a yellow rectangle in different ways.

You need
1 cm squared paper

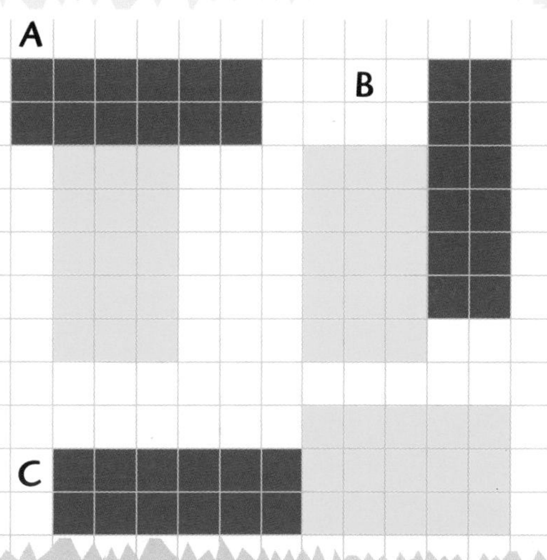

a Find the perimeter of each shape.

b Use 1 cm squared paper. Draw a similar blue and yellow shape

- that has the smallest perimeter
- that has the greatest perimeter.

c For each shape A to C, find another arrangement of blue and yellow rectangles to give the same perimeter.

3 This shape has an area of $14\,cm^2$ and a perimeter of 20 cm.

You need
CM 9

Small squares must join edge to edge.

a Use CM 9 to investigate different shapes with a perimeter of 20 cm.

b Find the area of each shape.

c Can you construct a shape that has a perimeter of 20 cm and an area less than $9\,cm^2$? Justify your answer.

1a Measure the diameter of these euro coins to the nearest millimetre.

b Copy and complete the table.

€ coin	mm	cm	m
1-cent			
2-cent			
5-cent			

2 Euro coins are placed end-to-end in straight lines. Find the approximate total length in metres of a line of:

a 100 1-cent coins **b** 1000 2-cent coins **c** 10 000 5-cent coins.

3 Euro 5-cent coins are placed end-to-end to make a straight line $\frac{1}{10}$ of a kilometre long. Find the total value of the coins, in cents.

4 The British Grand Prix for Formula One cars is held at Silverstone. The table shows how the length of one circuit has changed over the years.

You need a calculator

Year	Length of circuit
1948	2·9 miles
1975	2·932 miles
1991	3·2 miles
1997	3·194 miles

miles → × 8 → ÷ 5 → kilometres

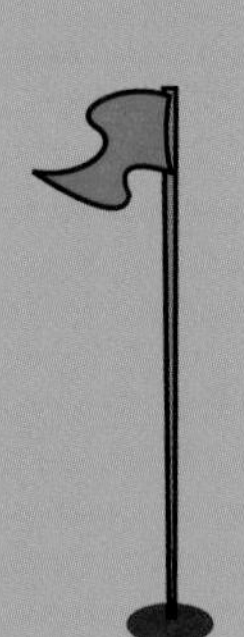

a For each year, find the length of one circuit in kilometres.

b The race is 60 laps of the circuit. Find the total distance, to 2 decimal places, of the 1997 race in:

- miles
- kilometres.

c In kilometres, how much longer was the race in 1991 than in 1948?

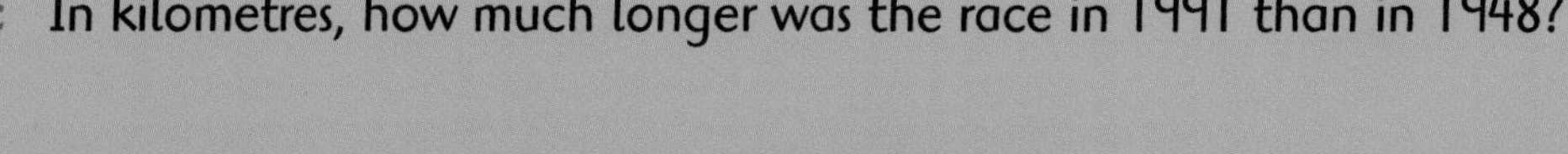

Unit 9 Use, read and write standard metric units of length, km, m, cm, mm, abbreviations and relationships. Convert larger to smaller units of length and vice versa. Know mile and kilometre equivalents. Suggest suitable units/equipment to estimate length.

You need
CM 10

1 BBC World transmits *Sports Today* at these times:

07:45 GMT | 12:45 GMT | 18:45 GMT

Find the local time for TV viewers to watch:

a the 12:45 broadcast in each of these cities:
- Singapore
- Oslo
- Tokyo
- Perth
- Nairobi
- Lima

b the 18:45 broadcast in each of these cities:
- New York
- Mexico City
- Santiago
- Rome
- Moscow
- San Francisco

2 The results of the British Open Golf Championship are announced in the 07:45 broadcast on Monday. Write the day and local time for *Sports Today* viewers in each of these cities:
- Wellington
- Hong Kong
- Johannesburg
- San Francisco
- Sydney
- Rio de Janeiro.

3 A sports car company has a London office and car showrooms in Paris, New York, Dallas and Cape Town. The weekday working hours are from 08:00 to 17:30 local time in each city.

a Find the range of local times during which the showroom manager in each of the four showrooms can phone the London office.

b Find the earliest local time for:
- the Paris showroom manager to call New York
- the Cape Town showroom manager to call Dallas.

1 An international cross-country race started at 12:30. The table shows the total time each country's team took to finish the race.

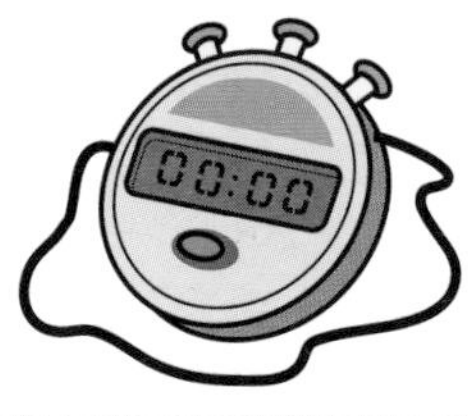

a List the countries in order of the time taken, starting with the winning team.

b Find the time difference between:
- the first and third teams
- the second and last teams.

Team	Total time
France	3 h 12 min
Great Britain	2 h 59 min
Ireland	3 h 14 min
Kenya	2 h 56 min
Morocco	3 h 4 min
Spain	3 h 7 min

2a On July 12 the sun rose at 4:57 am and set at 9:14 pm. For how long was it above the horizon?

b On July 12 the moon rose at 8:46 pm and set at 2:54 am. For how long could the moon be seen?

c The sun was above the horizon for 15 hours and 21 minutes on August 1. It set at 8:50 pm. When did it rise?

d On the same day the moon rose at 10:21 pm and set 6 hours and 55 minutes later. At what time did it set?

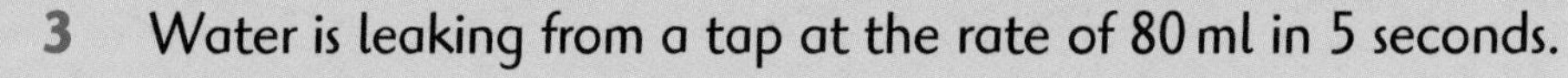

3 Water is leaking from a tap at the rate of 80 ml in 5 seconds.

a How long will it take to fill a 1 litre jug, in seconds? Round your answer to 1 decimal place.

b Using the same water-flow rate, find how much water is lost:
- in 1 hour
- in 1 day.

1 Play **Rectangle Hunt** with a partner.
The aim of the game is to find the positions of vertices of rectangles on your partner's grid.

You need
CM 11
red and blue coloured pencils

- Each draw three rectangles (1×4, 2×4, 2×2) on your left-hand grid on CM 11. Do not let your partner see them. The rectangles must not overlap.

- Take turns to suggest a coordinate pair for each other's grid. There are three possible responses:

Hit: the coordinate pair is part of a rectangle.

Vertex hit: the coordinate pair is the vertex of a rectangle.

Miss: the coordinate pair is not part of a rectangle.

- Mark your partner's response on your right-hand grid on CM 11.
Use blue for a hit, red for a vertex hit and pencil for a miss.
- The winner is the first player to find the vertices of all three rectangles.

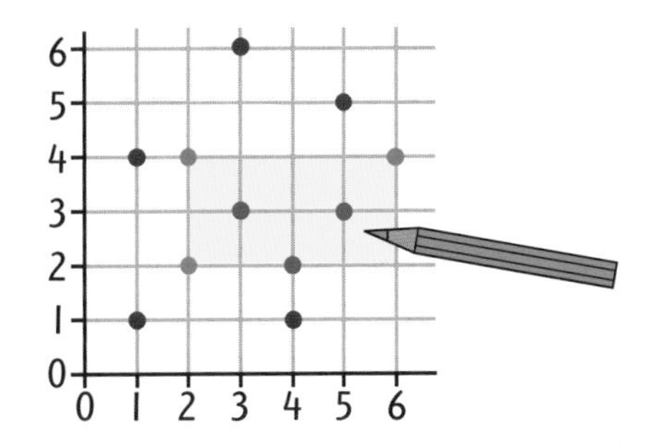

2 Make up your own rules for a coordinates game.

This rectangle has been translated 6 squares to the right and 3 squares down.

This could be shown as:

$x + 6$
$y - 3$

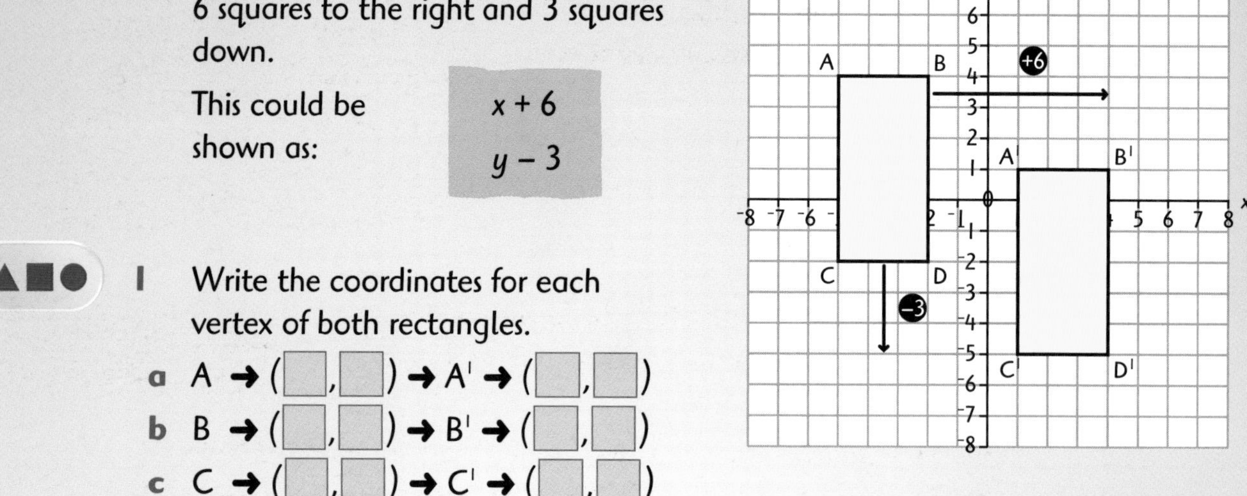

1 Write the coordinates for each vertex of both rectangles.

a A → (,) → A' → (,)

b B → (,) → B' → (,)

c C → (,) → C' → (,)

d D → (,) → D' → (,)

2 On CM 12, show where each shape will be after each of these translations:

You need
CM 12

▲ **a** $x - 5$ **b** $y + 7$ **c** $y + 5$ **d** $x + 6$

■ **a** $x - 7$ **b** $y + 5$ **c** $x - 4$, $y + 6$ **d** $x + 4$, $y + 4$

● **a** $x - 6$, $y - 2$ **b** $x + 8$, $y + 4$ **c** $x - 5$, $y + 4$ **d** $x + 2$, $y - 2$

3 Complete the table on CM 12 to record the coordinates of each shape and its new coordinates after the translation in question **2**.

Shape	Coordinates	Translation	New coordinates
a	(7, 3), (7, −2), (3, −2), (3, 3)		
b			

1 The table shows the heights of some tall buildings in London.
Write down $\frac{1}{100}$ of each actual height:
- in metres
- in centimetres.

Building	Actual height
Big Ben	96 m
Canary Wharf Tower	244 m
Tower 42	183 m
St Paul's Cathedral	112 m
Telecom Tower	187 m

2 At *Mini Europe* in Brussels some of the models of famous buildings are made to a scale of 1 m for every 200 m.

You need a calculator

a For each building in the table in question 1, find how tall its model would be if the scale of 1 m for every 200 m was used.

b On the scale of 1 m for every 200 m find, in millimetres, the height difference between:
- the tallest and the smallest model buildings
- the models of Tower 42 and the Telecom Tower.

c Using 1 inch ≈ 2·5 cm, convert the heights of the model buildings in question **2a** to the nearest inch.

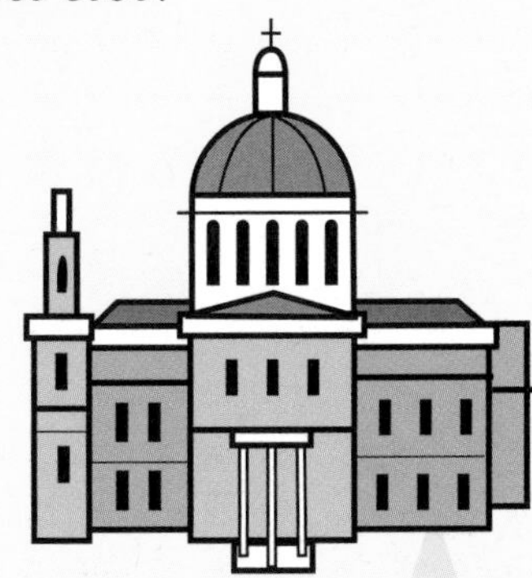

3 The Empire State Building in New York is 436 m tall.

a How much taller is it, in metres, than the combined heights of the Canary Wharf Tower and Tower 42?

b How many times taller, to one decimal place, is the Empire State Building than:
- Big Ben?
- St Paul's Cathedral?

4 At *Mini Europe*, a model boat makes the round trip from Canary Wharf to Big Ben in 7 minutes and 30 seconds.

a How many round trips will the model boat make:
- in 3 hours?
- from 10:00 am to 6:30 pm?

b How long, in hours, will the model boat take to make 1000 round trips?

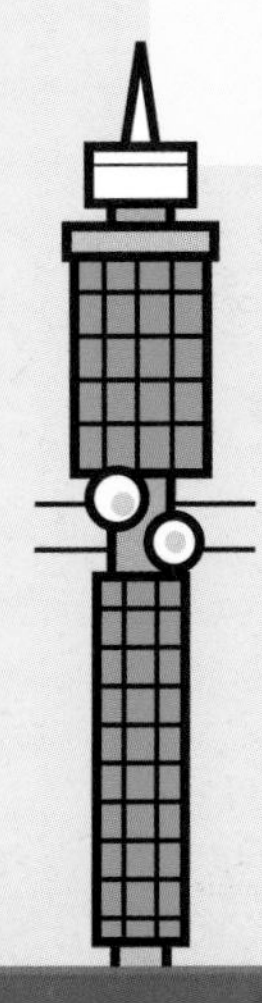

1a

1 kg ≈ 2·2 lb

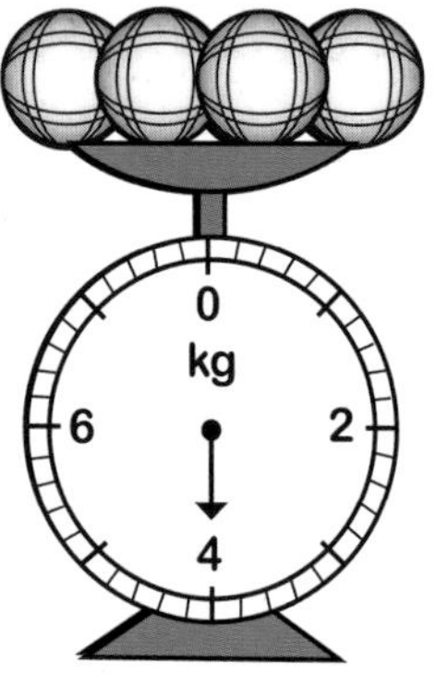

b

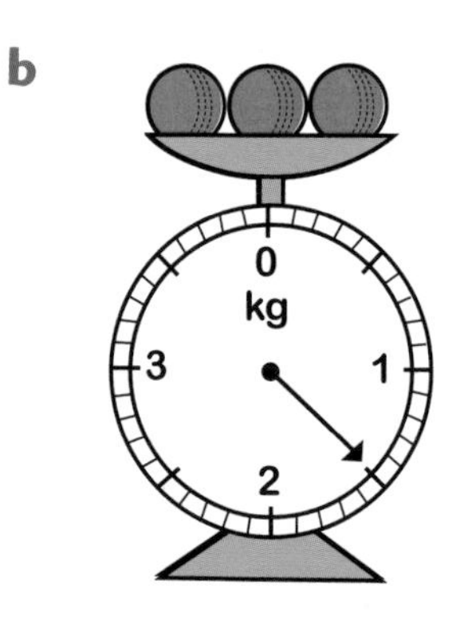

c

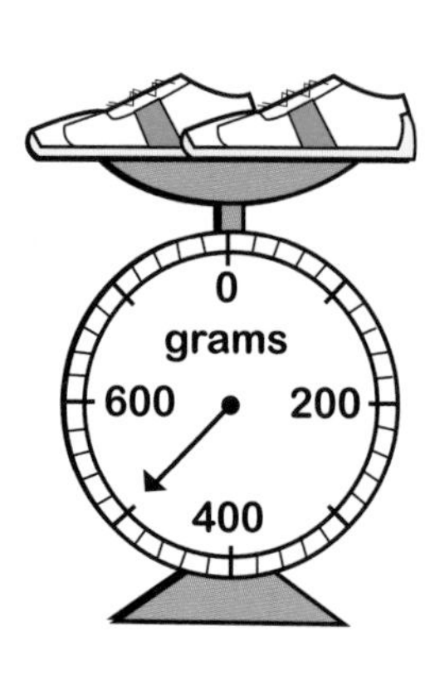

- Write the mass each scale shows, in kg and in lb.
- Find the mass of one item on each scale, in kg and in lb.

2 Use the **conversion scale** on CM 13 to convert these masses. Round your answers to the nearest $\frac{1}{4}$ lb or 10 g.

a $\frac{1}{4}$ lb **b** $1\frac{1}{4}$ lb **c** 800 g **d** 350 g **e** 2 lb

You need
CM 13
coloured pencils

3a Colour the triangles on CM 13 which show:
- grams approximately equal to $\frac{1}{2}$ lb, $\frac{3}{4}$ lb, $1\frac{1}{2}$ lb and $1\frac{3}{4}$ lb
- pounds (lb) heavier than $\frac{3}{4}$ kg
- masses lighter than $\frac{1}{2}$ lb.

Use a different colour for each set.

b The uncoloured triangle shows the mass of 1 litre of water. Complete the sentence: 1 litre of water has a mass of ☐.

4 Construct a graph on CM 13 to convert up to 18 litres to gallons.

Use the conversion 4·5 litres ≈ 1 gallon

5 Use your graph from question 4 to find how many gallons, to the nearest $\frac{1}{10}$ of a gallon, each container holds.

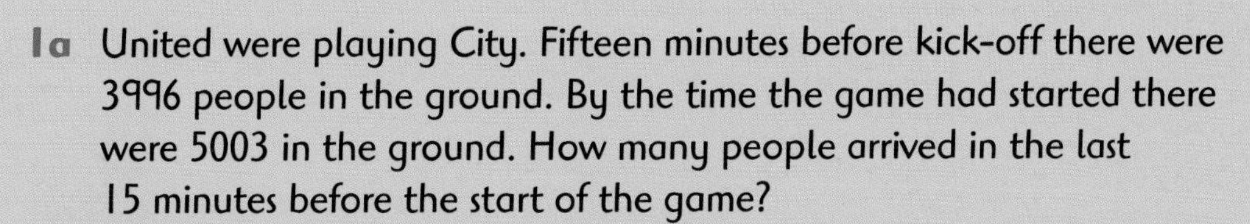

1a United were playing City. Fifteen minutes before kick-off there were 3996 people in the ground. By the time the game had started there were 5003 in the ground. How many people arrived in the last 15 minutes before the start of the game?

b The actual attendance was 6002. How many arrived after kick-off?

c 4896 spectators were standing in the stands. How many were sitting?

d Of the 6002 who attended the match, 1857 were children. How many were adults?

2 Find the two numbers, one from each half of the pitch, with:

a the largest difference

b the smallest difference

c a difference of 4229

d a difference that has two 4s and two 0s as its digits

e a difference with 11 as the sum of its digits.

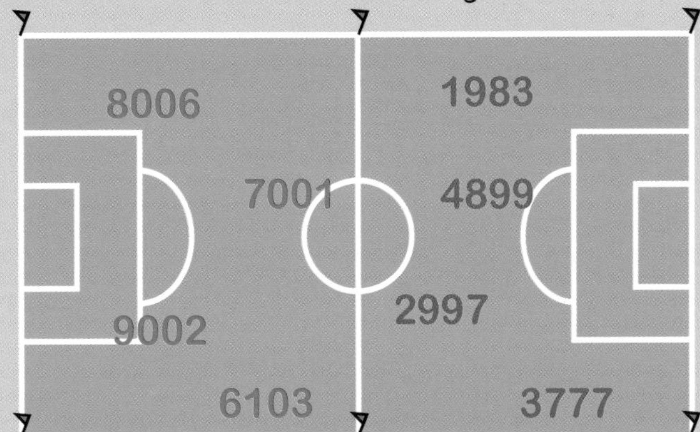

3 Investigate ways of completing the subtraction:

☐ 0 0 ☐ − ☐ ☐ 9 ☐ = 105

How many different ways can you find?

1 The table shows the results of a Year 6 cricket ball throwing competition.

Name	Distance in metres
Abigail	17·32
Babinder	14·5
Chris	15·17
Darrell	16
Eve	20·41

a By how many metres did the winner beat each of the other competitors?

b By how many metres was the shortest throw less than each of the other competitors' throws?

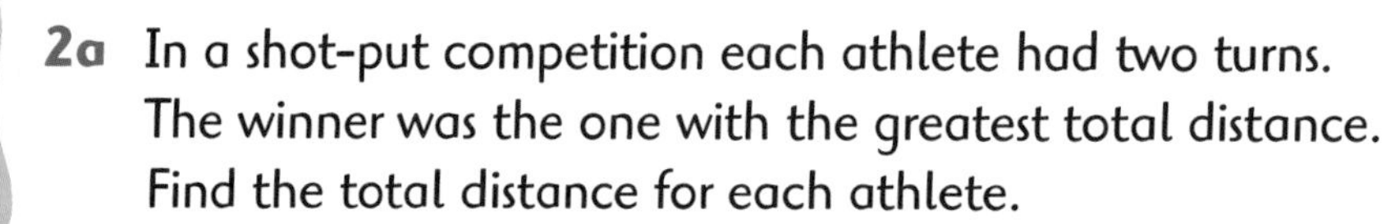

2a In a shot-put competition each athlete had two turns. The winner was the one with the greatest total distance. Find the total distance for each athlete.

Name	1st put in metres	2nd put in metres
Scott	6·36	7·33
Jones	5·08	6·94
Patel	6·71	7·36
Hussain	7·19	8·05
Greenwood	5·84	6·77

b By how many metres did the winner beat the runner-up?

3 Investigate different ways of using the digits 0 to 9 to complete these two calculations:

☐·☐ + ☐·☐☐ ☐·☐ − ☐·☐☐

a Try to make the sum of the two answers as large as you can.

b Try to make the difference between the two answers as small as you can.

Brisley Activity Centre

	Adult ticket	Child ticket (up to 12 years)	Family ticket (2 adults and 2 children)	Time per session
Swimming	£3·50	£2·25	£10·25	2·75h
Canoeing	£8·75	£6·50	£28·50	1·5h
Sailing	£12·95	£9·75	£40·75	1·2h
Rowing	£10·25	£8·10	£34·50	1·25h

▲■●

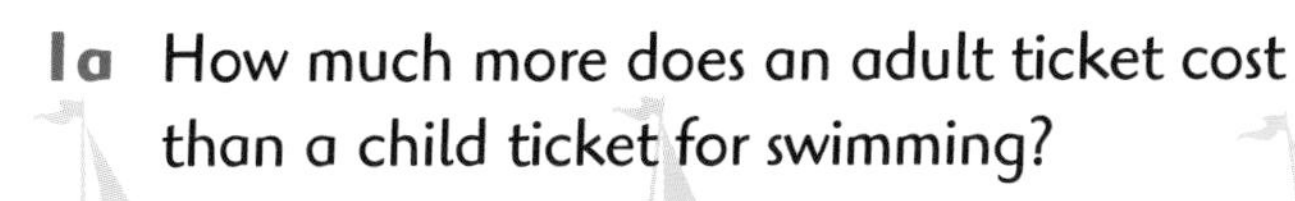

1a How much more does an adult ticket cost than a child ticket for swimming?

b Mary, who is 8 years old, goes canoeing with her mum. What is the total cost?

c Mr Harris takes his two children sailing. He pays with a £50 note. How much change does he get?

d Brisley Activity Centre has 18 sailing boats that take two people, 12 that take three people and 27 that take four people. How many people are sailing when all the boats are full?

■●

2a The Kumar family has 2 adults and 2 children. For each activity, how much do they save by buying a family ticket?

b Mr and Mrs Wallis pay £43·40 in total for two activities for the two of them. Which activities have they paid for?

c There are 30 rowing boats altogether, some for two and some for four people. When all the boats are in use there are 84 people rowing. How many boats carry two and how many carry four people?

●

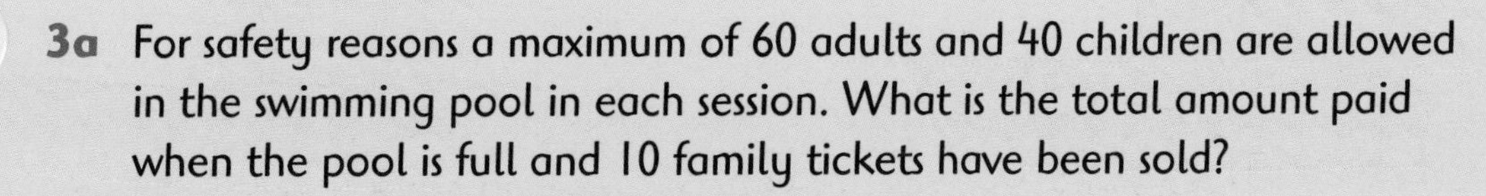

3a For safety reasons a maximum of 60 adults and 40 children are allowed in the swimming pool in each session. What is the total amount paid when the pool is full and 10 family tickets have been sold?

b The Samson family want to do every activity in one day. They arrive at Brisley at 09:00. Organise their day for them so that they have breaks and finish at 17:00.

Golf is scored by counting the number of strokes (hits) the player takes to complete one round of the course.
Golf courses are all different and some are easier than others.
The number of strokes expected from a top player to complete one round is called the 'par score' for the course.

1 This is the final scoreboard of a 4-day golf competition:

a What is the total score for each player?

b How many fewer strokes did Gill take than Chanda?

	Round			
	1	2	3	4
Gill	73	65	69	72
Martin	69	68	71	75
Anish	68	74	68	73
Chanda	70	73	70	72

2 Scores can also be shown as the number of strokes more (+) or less (–) than par.
The par score for this course is 72 strokes.
Copy and complete the table for the four players.

	Round			
	1	2	3	4
Gill	+1			
Martin	-3			
Anish	-4			
Chanda	-2			

3a In a season Martin played 26 golf tournaments. Each tournament had 4 rounds of 18 holes. How many holes of golf did Martin play in the season?

You need a calculator

b His total number of strokes for the 26 tournaments was 7072. What was his average (mean) score per round?

4 Use a calculator to find the missing numbers. Show your working.

a 38·6 + ☐ = 94·3

b ☐ × 2·6 = 46·28

c ☐ ÷ 5·2 = 3·7

d 91·4 – ☐ = 63·7

5 Two 1-place decimal numbers have the same two digits. The product of the numbers is 27·01. Use a calculator to find the two numbers.

Rule box

+8   -15   +2·5   -0·2   +140   -60   +0·6   -8·5

1 For each sequence below:
- find the correct rule from the box
- copy and complete the sequence.

a

15	17·5	20					

b

		2·5	3·1		4·3		

c

			50	35	20		

d

		45		28	19·5		

2 The middle number of each sequence is given. For each:
- choose a rule from the rule box
- copy and complete the sequence.

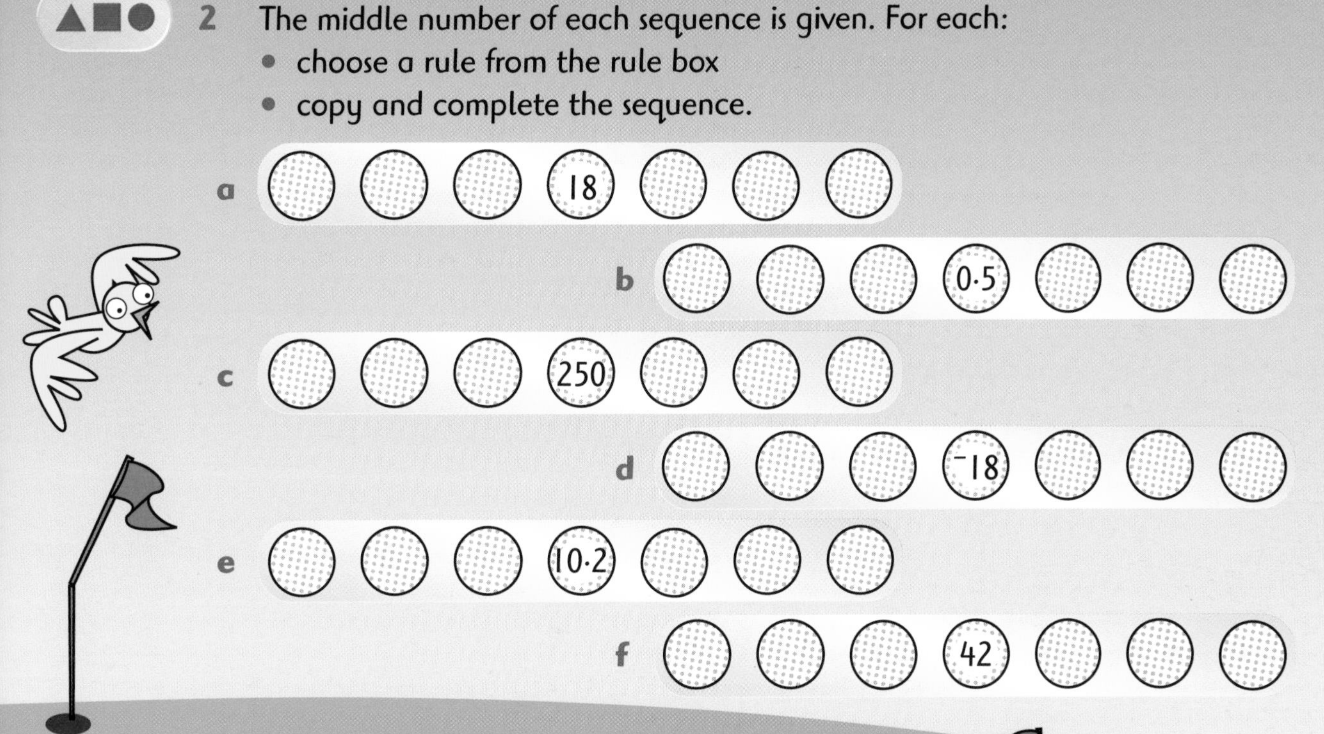

a 18

b 0·5

c 250

d ⁻18

e 10·2

f 42

3 The two end numbers of each sequence are given.
For each:
- work out the rule
- copy and complete the sequence.

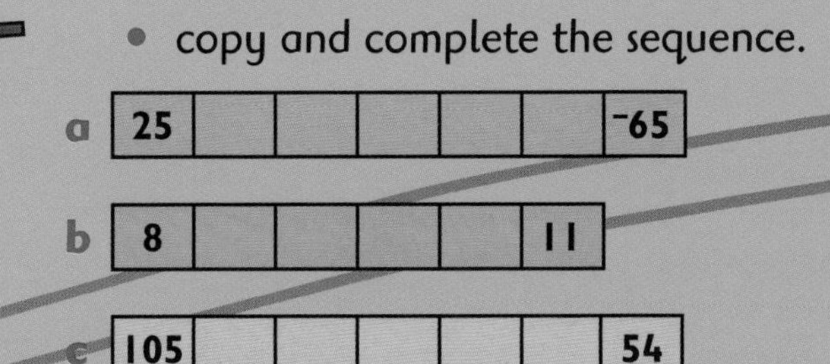

a

25						⁻65

b

8					11

c

105						54

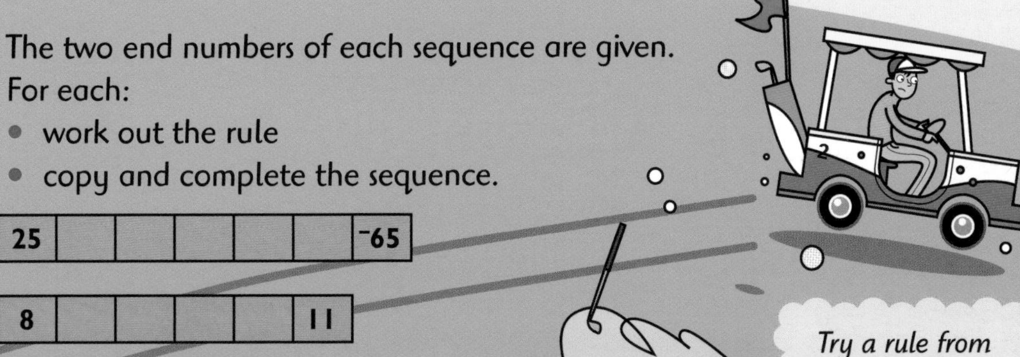

Try a rule from the rule box.

You need
CM 14
scissors
glue

1a Look at the 4 shapes on CM 14. Record the number of squares in each shape in the table.

Shape	1	2	3	4	
Number of squares	1	3			

b Predict how many squares there will be in the fifth shape.

c Draw the next four shapes in the sequence and complete the table.
Write about any patterns you see in the number sequence.

2 Carefully cut out all 8 shapes from CM 14 and arrange them in pairs to make squares.
Stick them onto paper.
Write about any patterns you notice.

You need
CM 15

3 The diagram below shows one-way streets and junctions. The car can only travel in the direction of the arrows. The number at each junction shows how many different routes the car can take to reach that point.

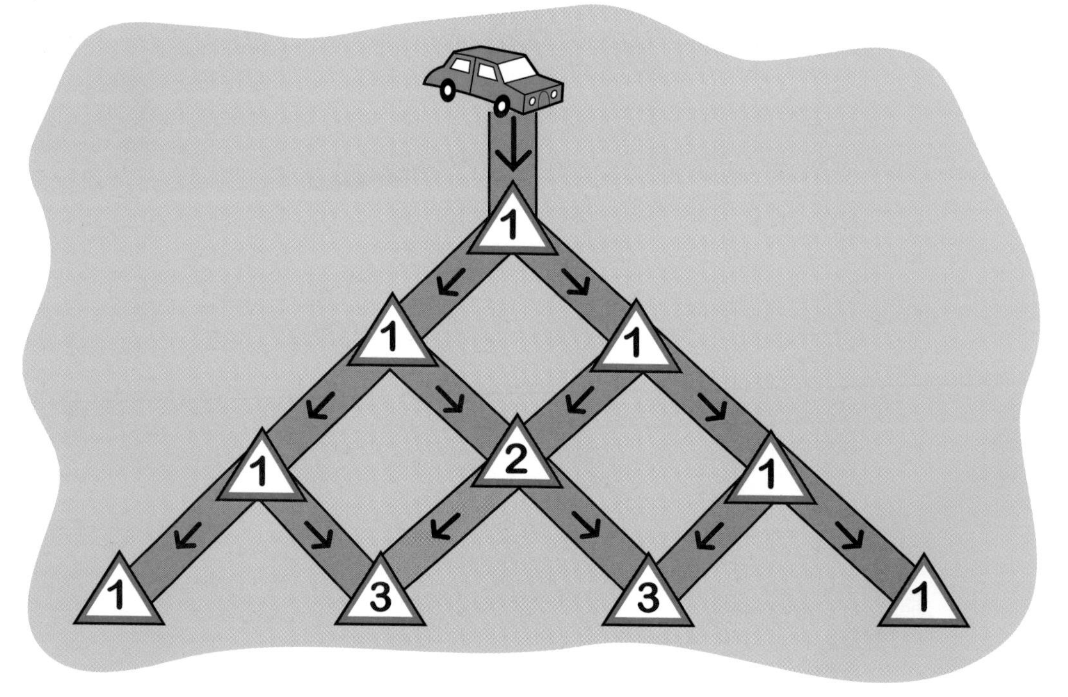

a Complete the numbers at the junctions on CM 15.

b Write about different patterns you can see.

1 Use sticks to make this shape sequence:

You need
sticks

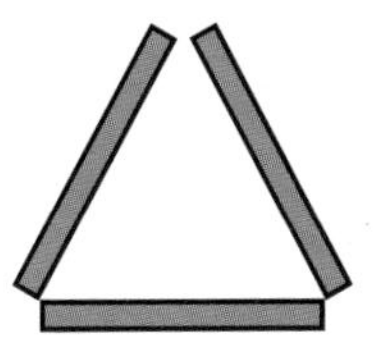
1st term

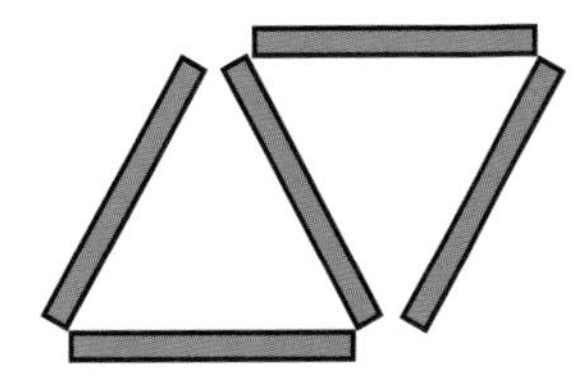
2nd term

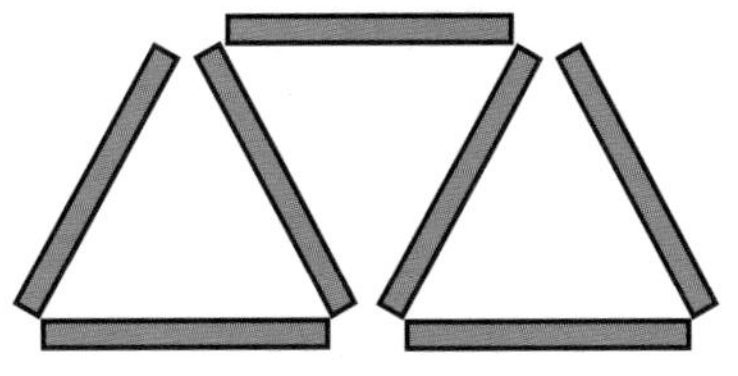
3rd term

Continue the shape sequence up to the 6th term.
Copy and complete the table.

Term number (T)	1	2	3	4	5	6
Sticks (S)	3	5				

Write about any patterns you notice in the results.

2 A formula for working out the number of sticks could be: $S = 2T + 1$
Use this formula to work out the number of sticks for these terms:

a 10th term **b** 18th term **c** 25th term **d** 100th term.

3 Make the next two terms in each of these shape sequences and record your results in a table.

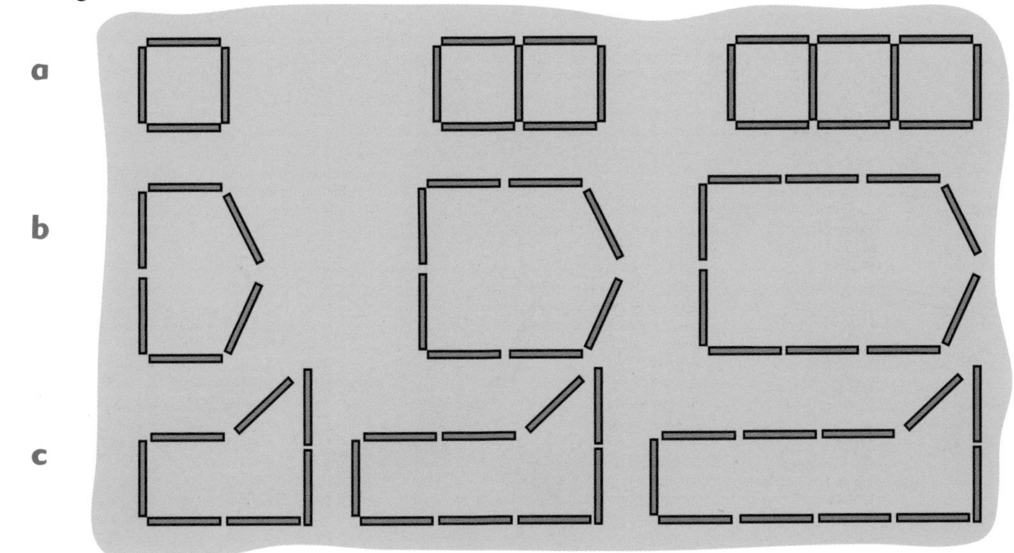

4 Work out a formula for each sequence in question **3**.

Term = T
Number of sticks = S

You need
CM 16

On the first day of Christmas my true love sent to me
A partridge in a pear tree.
On the second day of Christmas my true love sent to me
Two turtle doves and a partridge in a pear tree ...

1 All these presents were sent over 12 days:

1st day	A partridge in a pear tree
2nd day	Two turtle doves ...
3rd day	Three French hens ...
4th day	Four calling birds ...
5th day	Five gold rings ...
6th day	Six geese a-laying ...
7th day	Seven swans a-swimming ...
8th day	Eight maids a-milking ...
9th day	Nine ladies dancing ...
10th day	Ten lords a-leaping ...
11th day	Eleven pipers piping ...
12th day	Twelve drummers drumming ...

By the third day, 10 presents had already been sent:

Day	Running totals
1	1 partridge
2	2 partridges, 2 turtle doves
3	3 partridges, 4 turtle doves, 3 French hens

a How many presents in total were sent by the 12th day? Use CM 16 to record your results.

b Write about any patterns you can see in the triangle on CM 16.

Look at this subtraction pattern.
If you continue the pattern,
negative numbers appear.

$8 - 5 = 3$
$8 - 6 = 2$
$8 - 7 = 1$
$8 - 8 = 0$
$8 - 9 = {}^{-}1$
$8 - 10 = {}^{-}2$

You need
a calculator

1 Copy and continue these patterns:

a
$10 - 7 = 3$
$10 - 8 = 2$
$10 - 9 = 1$

b
$10 - 2 = 8$
$8 - 2 = 6$
$6 - 2 = 4$

c
$6 - 2 = 4$
$6 - 4 = 2$
$6 - 6 = 0$

d
$20 - 5 = 15$
$15 - 5 = 10$
$10 - 5 = 5$

What is the tenth number in each?
Use a calculator to check your answer.

2 Find the difference between each pair of numbers.

Use the number line to help.

a

b

c
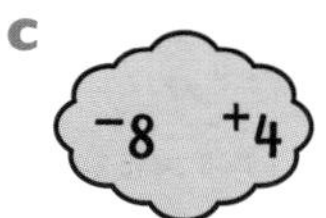

d

e

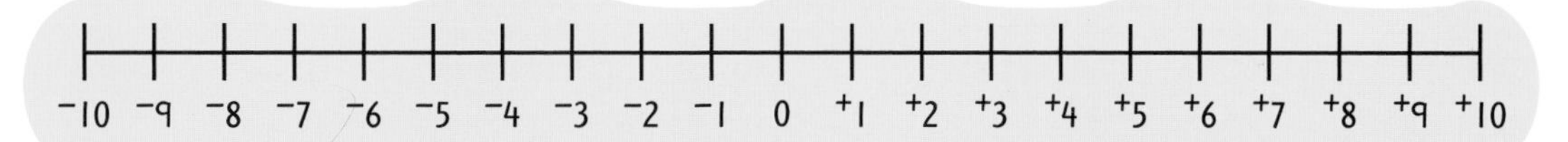

3 Each column, row and diagonal in this magic square adds to $^{-}12$.

$^{+}2$	$^{-}12$	$^{-}2$
$^{-}8$		0
$^{-}6$	$^{+}4$	$^{-}10$

a What is the missing centre number?

b Copy and complete these magic squares:

$^{-}5$		$^{-}1$
	$^{-}2$	
		$^{+}1$

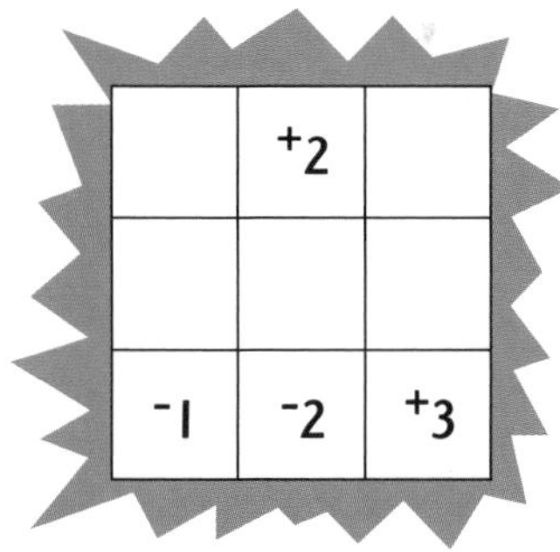

	$^{+}2$	
$^{-}1$	$^{-}2$	$^{+}3$

$^{-}8$		
$^{-}1$		
$^{-}6$		$^{-}2$

What does each column, row and diagonal add to?

c Make up a magic square for a partner to complete.

Questions 1 and 2 are about some times and distances achieved by athletes at the 2000 Sydney Olympic Games.

You need
CM 16

▲ **1a** Write these results in order on CM 16, starting with the gold medallists.

b Round each result to the nearest whole number.

Women's 400 m Final	
Lane 1 (MEX)	49·9 s
Lane 2 (GBR)	49·8 s
Lane 3 (AUS)	49·1 s
Lane 4 (JAM)	49·6 s
Lane 5 (RUS)	51·0 s
Lane 6 (GBR)	49·7 s
Lane 7 (NGR)	50·1 s
Lane 8 (RSA)	50·0 s

Men's Javelin Final	
Athlete 1 (GBR)	89·9 m
Athlete 2 (GRE)	86·5 m
Athlete 3 (CUB)	83·3 m
Athlete 4 (GER)	87·8 m
Athlete 5 (GER)	85·8 m
Athlete 6 (RUS)	88·7 m
Athlete 7 (FIN)	86·6 m
Athlete 8 (CZE)	90·2 m

■● **2a** Write these results in order on CM 16, starting with the gold medallists.

b Round each result to the nearest tenth.

Men's 100 m Final	
Lane 1 (TRI)	9·99 s
Lane 2 (GBR)	10·13 s
Lane 3 (GBR)	10·08 s
Lane 4 (StK)	10·17 s
Lane 5 (USA)	10·09 s
Lane 6 (USA)	9·87 s
Lane 7 (BAR)	10·04 s

Women's Long Jump Final	
Athlete 1 (GER)	6·99 m
Athlete 2 (BAH)	6·59 m
Athlete 3 (USA)	6·92 m
Athlete 4 (RUS)	6·83 m
Athlete 5 (ITA)	6·93 m
Athlete 6 (RUS)	6·79 m
Athlete 7 (GER)	6·74 m
Athlete 8 (HUN)	6·58 m

● **3** Six children raced their snails to see which could go furthest in half an hour. Distances were measured to the nearest millimetre.

a Write the snails' distances in order, starting with the longest distance.

b If the distances are rounded to the nearest tenth, does it alter the result?

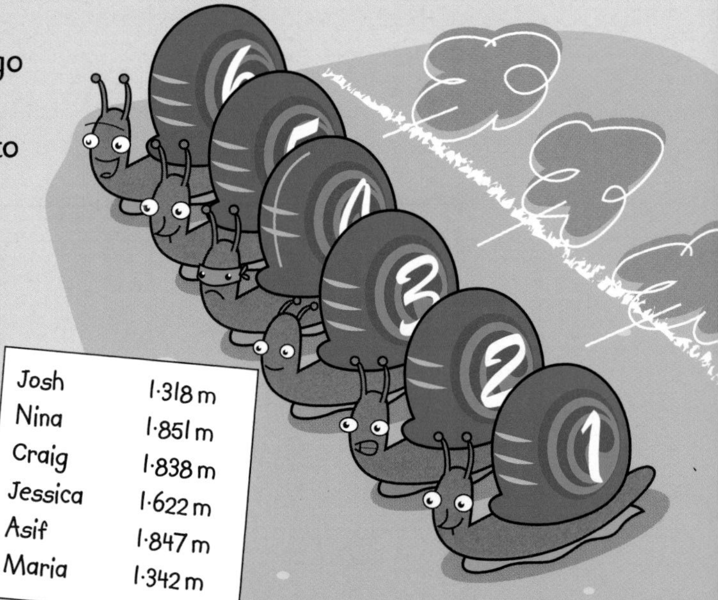

Josh	1·318 m
Nina	1·851 m
Craig	1·838 m
Jessica	1·622 m
Asif	1·847 m
Maria	1·342 m

Unit 1 Order a mixed set of numbers as measurements with up to three decimal places.
Round a number with two decimal places to the nearest tenth or nearest whole number.

1a Find the score for each child.

b Who wins a prize?

c Find all the different pairs of blue and red skittles that would win a prize.

2 Multiply each number on a balloon by 5, 50 and 500.

0·03 0·6 5·7

3 Use the doubling machine to multiply each number by 4.

a 7 **b** 3·2 **c** 0·9 **d** 0·85

Show your working.

Input → DOUBLE → DOUBLE → Output

4a Use the digits 1, 2 and 3 to complete this decimal number in 6 different ways. □□·□

b Divide each number by 10. What is the total of the 6 answers?

5a Use the digits 1, 2 and 3 once each to complete this decimal number in 6 different ways. 0·□□□

b Multiply each number by 10. What is the total of the 6 answers?

6 What do you notice about your answers to questions **4b** and **5b**? Explain.

A record company is making CDs and DVDs. All the tracks on a CD or DVD will be the same length.

1 How many minutes of music will there be if there are:

a 10 tracks each 2·25 minutes long?

b 80 tracks each 1·75 minutes long?

c 15 tracks each 2·2 minutes long?

d 100 tracks each 1·98 minutes long?

2 Calculate the length of each track in minutes and seconds for:

You need a calculator

a a 10-track CD with 1 hour 10 minutes of music

b a 40-track DVD with 2 hours 10 minutes of music

c a 30-track CD with 1 hours 3 minutes of music

d a 20-track CD with 35 minutes of music.

3 For each CD or DVD in question **2**, what would be the total time, in minutes, between the start of the first track and the end of the last track, if an interval of 3 seconds is placed between each track?

4 Complete the spider diagram on CM 17 using related number facts.

You need CM 17

1 Kim is planting seeds in rows.
She plants 6 beans all the same distance apart in a row 100 cm long.

There are 5 gaps between 6 seeds. Each gap must be 20 cm long, since 100 ÷ 5 = 20.

She still has these seeds to plant:

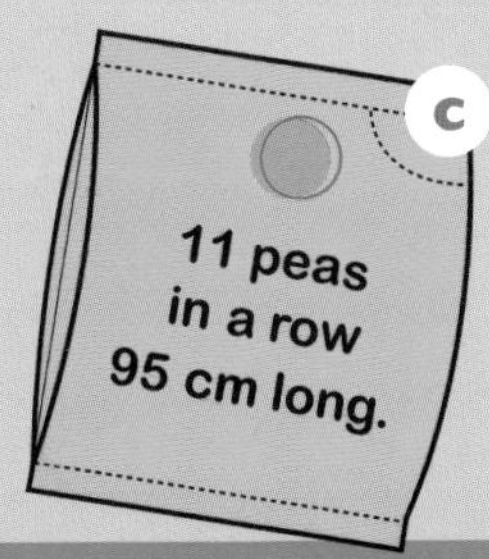

For each packet find:

- the number of gaps between seeds
- the length of each gap.

Write any remainder as a decimal.

Use a calculator to check your answers.

2 Write the answer to each division in 3 ways:

- with a remainder
- as a mixed number
- as a decimal number.

a $54 \div 4$ b $37 \div 8$ c $74 \div 5$ d $123 \div 10$

Check using a calculator.

3a Use whole numbers to complete this division in 3 different ways:

$\square \div \square = 6{\cdot}4$

b Use what you found in **a** to write 3 different ways to complete each division.

- $\square \div \square = 12{\cdot}8$
- $\square \div \square = 3{\cdot}2$

Explain how you found the ways.
Check each division using the inverse operation and a calculator.

For each question, write the calculation and show your working.

You need a calculator

1a Rick's mum needs 460 tiles.
How many boxes does she need?
How much does she pay altogether to the nearest pound?

b Mary's dad pays a total of £189·75 for 33 paving stones. What is the cost of one paving stone?

c Mr Chung has a £50 note.
How many rolls of wallpaper can he buy?
How much more money does he need to buy one more roll?

d Bess's parents are building an extension. They estimate they will need 5000 bricks. There are 128 bricks in a crate.
How many crates should they order?

2 Choose a number from a paint pot and a number from a brush.
Divide your paint pot number by the brush number.
Use a calculator to find the answer rounded to one decimal place.
Do this 10 times.

3 Find 3 different ways to complete this division.

☐☐☐ ÷ ☐

The answer has at least 2 decimal places and, when rounded to one decimal place, is 23·1.

1 Complete each calculation.

a $(3 + 4) \times 6 =$ ☐ b $7 \times (9 - 2) =$ ☐ c $(8 + 1) \times (8 - 1) =$ ☐

2 Use the digits 1, 2 and 3 to complete each calculation.

a $(\square + \square) \times \square = 9$

b $\square \times (\square - \square) = 4$

c $\square - (\square \times \square) = 1$

3a Choose a number from each shape. Use these numbers to complete each calculation.

3 2 4

- ■ × (● + ▲) =
- (■ × ●) + ▲ =

b What is the difference between the 2 answers in part **a**?

c Sol says:

One of the numbers in the triangle (8, 9 or 10) is a factor of the difference.

Is he correct? Test what Sol says using other numbers from the shapes.

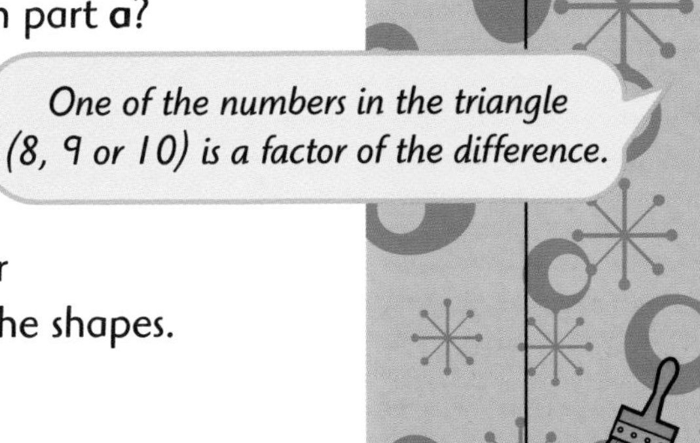

4 The 4 missing whole numbers in this calculation are different and are less than 6.

$(\square - \square) \times (\square + \square) = 12$

Find all the possible solutions.

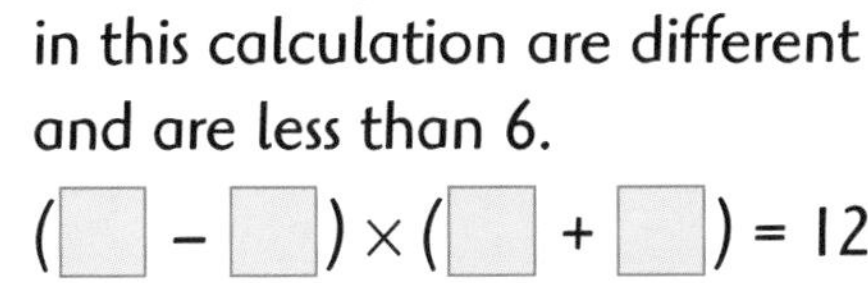

You can use a calculator to help.

You need a calculator

1 Each class at Hestam Primary School is putting on a play. The table shows the numbers of tickets sold and the number of chairs in each row.

The rows of chairs are filled up one at a time.

Class	Day	Number of tickets	Number of chairs in each row
2	Monday	127	7
3	Tuesday	138	8
4	Wednesday	115	6
5	Thursday	155	9
6	Friday	166	9

a For each day work out:

- how many rows are completely full
- how many rows are needed altogether
- the fraction of the final row that is occupied.

b For each day, write as a mixed number the number of occupied rows.

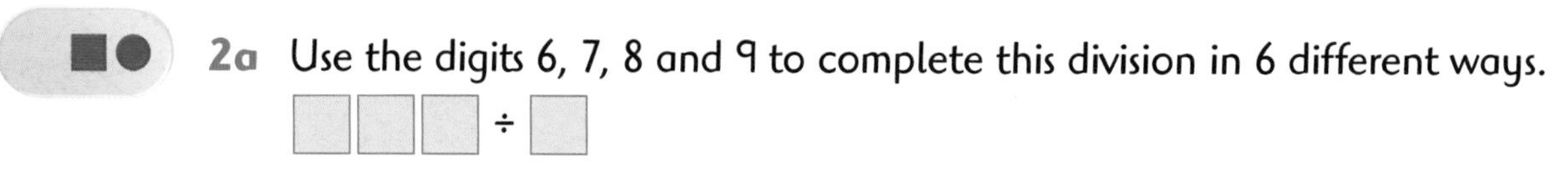

2a Use the digits 6, 7, 8 and 9 to complete this division in 6 different ways.

☐☐☐ ÷ ☐

Write each answer with a remainder and as a mixed number.

b Write the 6 answers in order, smallest first.

c Write the division that has:

- the largest possible answer
- the smallest possible answer.

3 Use 4 different digits to complete this division so that the answer is a 1-place decimal number.

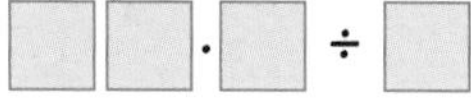

☐☐.☐ ÷ ☐

Find 5 different ways of doing this.

4 Use the digits 4 to 9 twice each to make this statement true.

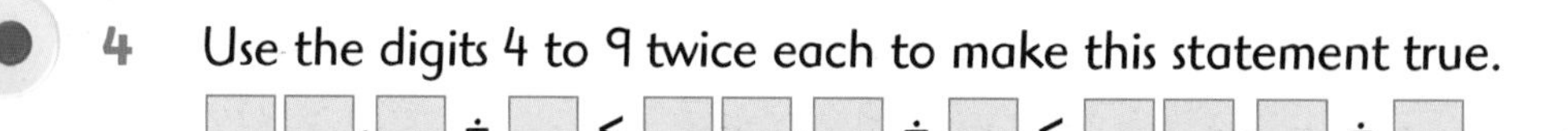

☐☐.☐ ÷ ☐ < ☐☐.☐ ÷ ☐ < ☐☐.☐ ÷ ☐

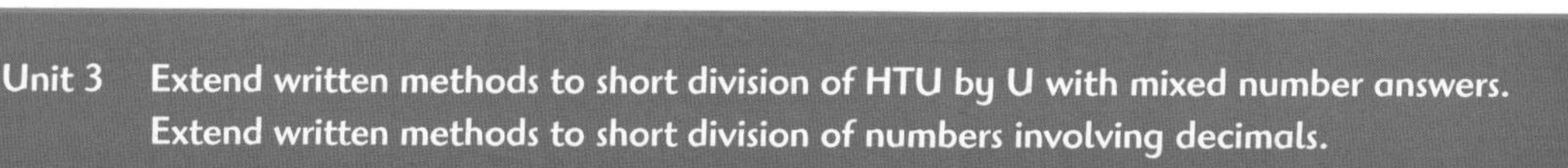

1 For each night of the Firework Fiesta, the cost of a ticket was different.

Day	Number of tickets sold	Cost of a ticket
Monday	327	£6
Tuesday	291	£10
Wednesday	346	£12
Thursday	485	£17
Friday	468	£20
Saturday	593	£25

a Find an approximation for the total amount taken in ticket sales each day.

b Calculate the exact amount taken each day.

2a Jade uses the digits 1, 2, 3, 4 and 5 to make the multiplication 123×45. Find the answer to her multiplication.

b Use the same 5 digits to make a 3-digit by 2-digit multiplication that has an answer:
- greater than Jade's
- smaller than Jade's.

3a Look at what Mei says. Is it true?

b Does the difference between 258×58 and 285×85 have 9 and 3 as factors?

c What do you notice about the numbers in parts **a** and **b**? Predict a pair of 3-digit by 2-digit multiplications with a difference that has 9 and 4 as factors. Test your prediction.

▲■● **1** The table shows the number of days the Sea Life Centre was open and the total number of visitors each month for a year.

Month	Jan	Feb	Mar	Apr	May	Jun	Jul	Aug	Sept	Oct	Nov	Dec
Days open	12	21	23	25	29	30	31	31	27	26	22	24
Number of visitors	468	504	575	650	812	870	992	961	729	598	528	672

For each of the first 6 months, find the average number of visitors to the Centre for each day it was open.

■● **2a** In July, the ratio of children to adult visitors was 3 to 1. What was the average number of children per day?

b In November, 25% of the visitors were adults. What was the average number of children on each day that the Centre was open?

● **3** Gail notices that all the digits in this calculation are different.

4 6 8 ÷ 1 2 = 3 9

Try to find other 3-digit by 2-digit divisions that have 7 different digits.

Estimate the answer to each question, then use a calculator to check.

You need
a calculator

Ice World

Mon	10:00 – 15:30	£4·20
	20:30 – 22:30 (D*)	£5·60
Tues	10:00 – 15:30	£4·20
Wed	10:00 – 15:30	£4·20
	20:30 – 22:30 (D*)	£5·60
Thurs	10:00 – 15:30	£4·20
Fri	10:00 – 15:30	£4·20
	20:30 – 22:30 (D*)	£6·40
Sat	10:00 – 12:30	£4·80
	14:30 – 17:00 (D*)	£5·60
	20:30 – 22:30 (D*)	£6·40
Sun	10:00 – 12:00	£4·80
	14:00 – 16:00	£4·80

D* disco sessions

Skate hire (per person)	£1·40
Spectators (day)	75p
Spectators (evening)	£1·20
Family tickets (4 people including at least 1 adult)	
Weekend	£18·00
Weekday	£15·00

▲ **1** At Ice World on Monday they took £462 for skate hire.
How many people hired skates?

2 Dean went with 5 friends to the disco session on Saturday afternoon.

a What was the total admission charge?

b They bought a can of drink each, at a cost of £2·70 altogether.
What was the cost of each can, in pence?

c How much did it cost for them all to hire skates?

d What was the total cost of their outing?

■● **3** Hester went to Ice World with 11 friends during the day on Wednesday. The total cost for entry and skate hire was £52·65.
All the skaters hired skates.
How many went as:

- skaters?
- spectators?

4 One evening, 268 people went to Ice World for a competition, in coaches with 35 seats each.

a How many coaches were needed?

b The coach company charged £308·20.
How much did each person's coach ticket cost?

c If the coaches had been full and the cost of each ticket had stayed the same, how much more money would have been taken?

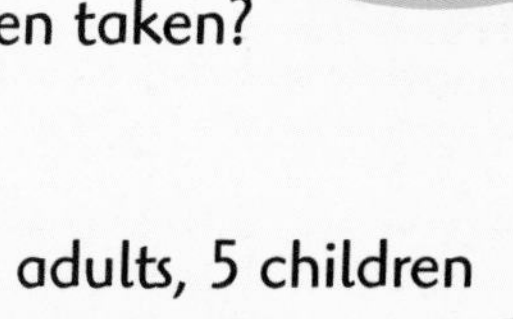

● **5** Find the cheapest time to visit Ice World for a group of 2 adults, 5 children and 1 spectator. Which combination of tickets gives the best deal?

Work with a partner.

You need
CM 18
a calculator
colouring pencils

The northern part of Lake Garda in Italy is very popular for water sports. It also provides a living for fishermen.

The Lake Garda Authority is planning to divide up an area 5 km by 2 km at the northern end of the lake. Each water sport and the fishermen will have their own section.

1a What is the approximate area of the part of the lake that will be divided up?

b The table shows the percentages of the total area each sport needs. The rest will be left for fishing.

- Find the area available for each sport in square kilometres.
- Find the area left for fishing.

sailing	25%
windsurfing	20%
waterskiing	15%
canoeing	5%
diving	5%
swimming	5%

2 Using the information below, think about where each sport area might be, and plan the areas on CM 18.

Each activity needs access from the banks of the lake.

Canoes are good in shallow water around the edge of the lake.

The area reserved for fishing is at least 1 km from the northern shore of the lake.

The waterskiers would like their area to be at least 2 km long.

3 What if your plan could use the next 0·5 km of the lake too? How would your design change?

You need a calculator

1 Change these Italian prices in euros (€) to pounds.
Try to do each one without the calculator first, then check.

€1·43 = £1
Divide the euro price by 1·43 to find the price in pounds.
Round your answer to the nearest penny.

a €1·43 b €2·86 c €14·30 d €7·15 e €28·60

2 Brad and Kylie both had a half-hour waterskiing lesson. It cost them €9·95 each.

a How much did it cost for them both in euros?

b How much is that in pounds?

3 Work with a partner. Nadia has 2 hours to enjoy her favourite watersports: swimming, canoeing and windsurfing. Her gran has given her £30 worth of euros to spend. What could she do? Show your working clearly.

4 Cara and Peter hired a sailing dinghy for an hour at a cost of €35·75.

a How much is that in pounds?

b They had £30 worth of euros to spend. How many euros did they have left? Show your working clearly.

5 Rafiq wants to have at least 2 hours of diving lessons, and he needs to hire a wetsuit. He has £50 to spend. Does he have enough?

6 You have £50 worth of euros to spend on watersports. Which sport or sports would you choose? Try to have as little left over as possible. Show your working clearly.

1a Cut out 6 identical squares.
Write the length of the sides in mm.

b Place the squares in a row with edges touching.
Write a calculation to calculate the perimeter.

c Find other ways to arrange the squares to make a shape with the same perimeter.
Write a calculation to calculate the perimeter each time.

You need
a calculator
paper
scissors

2a  and stand for different whole numbers in each puzzle.

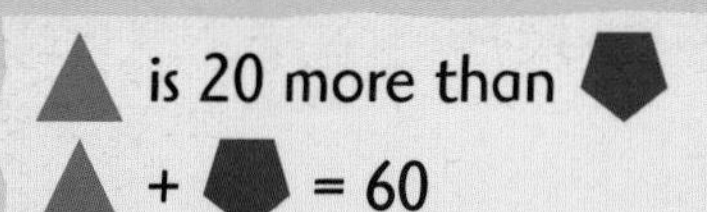

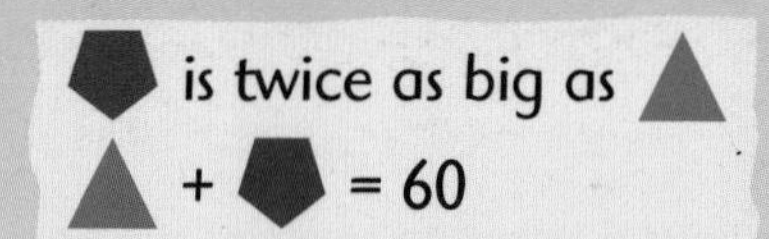

Talk to your partner about the puzzles and how to solve them.

b Make up similar puzzles to swap.

3a Use dotty paper to investigate irregular polygons with right-angled corners and a perimeter of 16 cm.

b Write an efficient way to check the perimeter each time.

You need
square dotty paper

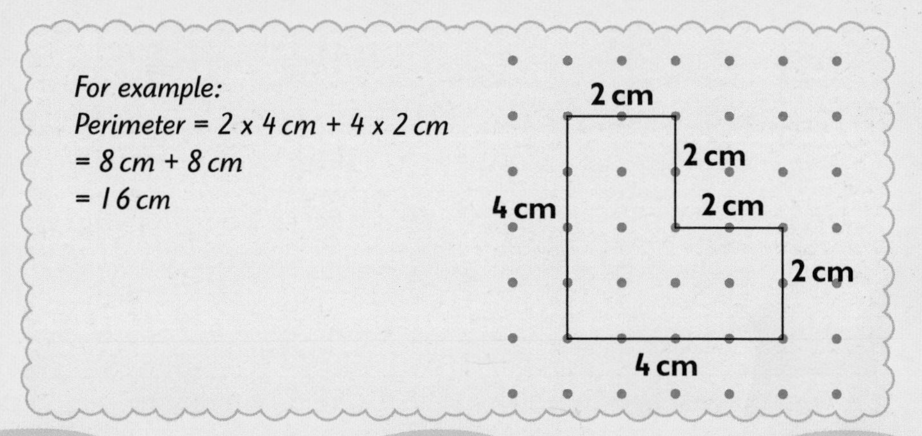

4a Imagine you had a length of rope 16 m long with loops for pegs every metre.
What regular polygons could you make with a perimeter of 16 m?

b What regular polygons could you make with a rope 20 m long?

c Investigate what length of rope up to 50 m would let you make the greatest number of regular polygons.

▲ **1** Work with a partner to make a set of 6 proper fractions. Include different fifths, tenths, quarters and hundredths.

For example: $\frac{2}{4}$ $\frac{29}{100}$ $\frac{7}{10}$ $\frac{3}{4}$ $\frac{4}{5}$ $\frac{73}{100}$

You need
a metre rule
a calculator

a Predict their order, from smallest to largest.

b Find the fractions in hundredths on a metre rule and write them in order, from smallest to largest.

c Use a calculator to find the fractions as decimal fractions and check your answer to **b**.

▲■ **2a** Find the equivalent fraction with denominator 30 for:

You need
A3 paper

$\frac{1}{3} = \frac{2}{6} = \frac{3}{9} = \ldots$ $\frac{1}{5} = \frac{2}{10} = \frac{3}{15} = \ldots$ $\frac{1}{6} = \frac{2}{12} = \frac{3}{18} = \ldots$

b Write the equivalent fraction with denominator 30 for:

$\frac{2}{3}$ $\frac{5}{6}$ $\frac{3}{5}$

c Draw a line 30 cm long. Label one end 0 and the other 1.
- Label $\frac{15}{30}$ $(\frac{1}{2})$. Write on the equivalent fractions from **b**.
- List the fractions from **b** in order, from largest to smallest.

■● **3** Look at these pairs of fractions:

$\frac{2}{5}$ $\frac{3}{10}$ $\frac{1}{2}$ $\frac{7}{14}$ $\frac{5}{6}$ $\frac{4}{5}$ $\frac{7}{12}$ $\frac{2}{3}$

$\frac{2}{3}$ $\frac{3}{4}$ $\frac{3}{5}$ $\frac{2}{3}$ $\frac{1}{3}$ $\frac{2}{7}$ $\frac{2}{5}$ $\frac{3}{8}$

a Change both fractions in each pair into equivalents with a common denominator.

b For each pair, use <, = or > to write a true number sentence.

For example: $\frac{1}{3}$ $\frac{1}{4}$

a $\frac{4}{12}$ $\frac{3}{12}$ **b** $\frac{1}{3} > \frac{1}{4}$

● **4a** Place these fractions in the correct order on a number line.

The line does not need to have an exact scale.

$\frac{2}{5}$ $\frac{3}{10}$ $\frac{1}{2}$ $\frac{5}{6}$ $\frac{4}{5}$

b Find at least one fraction that lies between each pair on the number line. Try to find the one with the smallest possible denominator each time.

These young athletes are competing in a triathlon event.
They each have to swim 400 m, cycle 10 km and run 2·5 km.

1 Find the mass of each competitor.

a **Alisha** $\frac{3}{5}$ **of 100 kg**

b **Becky** $\frac{9}{10}$ **of Alisha's mass**

c **Charlie** $\frac{8}{9}$ **of Becky's mass**

2 Find out how far each competitor has gone in this stage:

a $\frac{7}{10}$ **of stage completed**

b $\frac{2}{5}$ **of stage completed**

c $\frac{3}{5}$ **of stage completed**

3 How much water is left in each bottle at the end of the event?

a **holds 750 ml** $\frac{2}{3}$ **full**

b **holds 500 ml** $\frac{3}{20}$ **full**

c **holds 1·5 l** $\frac{4}{15}$ **full**

4 What positions did they finish in?

a **Group 1**
- 22 competitors
- Alisha behind exactly $\frac{1}{2}$ of the competitors

b **Group 2**
- 42 competitors
- Becky behind exactly $\frac{4}{7}$ of the competitors

c **Group 3**
- 36 competitors
- Charlie behind exactly $\frac{7}{9}$ of the competitors

5 Find how many boys and how many girls were in each group.

a **Group 1** $\frac{1}{11}$ were girls

b **Group 2** $\frac{2}{3}$ were girls

c **Group 3** $\frac{5}{12}$ were boys

1 Play with a partner.
Shuffle the cards and take 6 each.
Take turns to:

- throw the dice to give a denominator (bottom number)
- choose one of your cards to be the numerator (top number)
- turn your improper (top-heavy) fraction into a mixed number
- use the whole-number part for your score.

Use a different card each time.

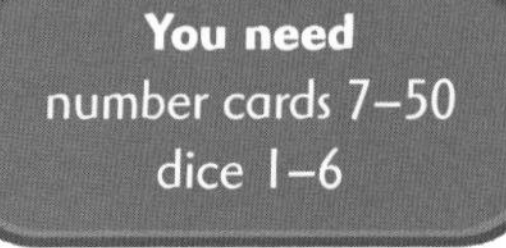

2 Alisha's triathlon time was 100 minutes.
Becky took $1\frac{1}{4}$ times as long and Charlie took $1\frac{1}{10}$ times as long.
What were the times for Becky and Charlie?

3 Charlie bought a new cycle helmet last year for £15.
Becky wants one like Charlie's but it now costs $1\frac{1}{3}$ times as much.
Find how much she will have to pay:

You need
a calculator

a working mentally $1\frac{1}{3} \times £15 = (1 \times £15) + (\frac{1}{3} \times £15) =$

b using a calculator. $1\frac{1}{3} \times £15 = \frac{4}{3} \times £15 = £(15 \div 3) \times 4 =$

4 Predict which product is the largest.

Use a calculator to check.

5 Distances for a standard triathlon are:

- swim 1500 m
- cycle 42 km
- run 12 km

Compare each standard distance with those at the top of page 58.
What mixed numbers do you need to multiply by to get the standard triathlon distances?

▲ **1a** Look at the labels on different clothes. Record the percentages of different fibres in each fabric: cotton, viscose, acrylic, polyester, wool…

You need
clothes made from different fabrics

b Write the percentages for each label as decimals and fractions. For example:

cotton $60\% = 0{\cdot}6 = \frac{6}{10} = \frac{3}{5}$ viscose $40\% = 0{\cdot}4 = \frac{4}{10} = \frac{2}{5}$

▲■ **2** Find these percentages mentally.

You need
a calculator

a	10% of 50	5% of 50	15% of 50
b	10% of 200	1% of 200	11% of 200
c	10% of 250	40% of 250	60% of 250
d	10% of 1500	1% of 1500	19% of 1500

Use the [%] key on the calculator to check the final answer in each part.

■● **3** Play with a partner.
Put the percentage cards in a pile face down.
Take turns to:

- throw 3 dice and make a 3-digit number
- turn over a percentage card and estimate that percentage of your number.

Check each other's estimates on a calculator.

- Score 1 if your estimate is within 20 of the exact answer.
- Score 2 if your estimate is within 10 of the exact answer.
- Score 3 if your estimate is within 5 of the exact answer.

You need
a calculator
3 dice
percentage cards
3%, $12\frac{1}{2}$%, 21%, $33\frac{1}{3}$%, 47%, 59%, $66\frac{2}{3}$%, 73%, 99%, 200%

● **4** Read these instructions to the end before you start.

- Draw 3 number lines.
- On the first line, position the percentage cards from question **3**.
- On the second line, write the decimal equivalents.
- On the third line, write the fraction equivalents in their simplest form.

You need
A3 paper

For example:

0 — 73% — 200%

0 — 0·73 — 2

0 — $\frac{73}{100}$ — 2

Unit 5a Express simple fractions as decimals and percentages.
Find simple percentages of whole number quantities.
Develop calculator skills and use a calculator effectively.

Shapes made from 4 identical squares are called tetrominoes.

Make your own set of tetrominoes for these activities, using cm squared paper. There are 5 different shapes.

You need
cm squared paper
scissors
ruler

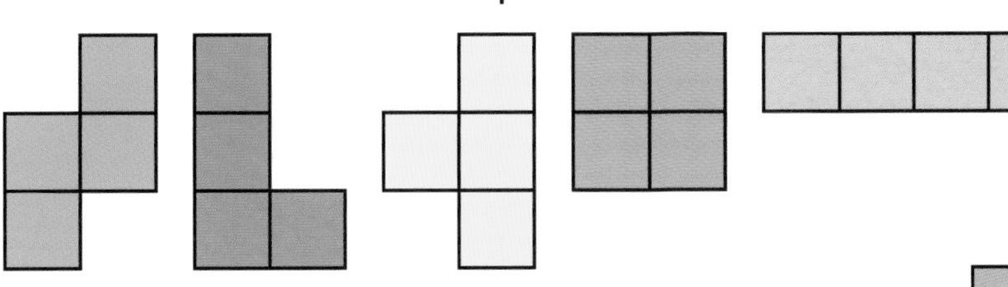

This design was made by rotating one of the tetrominoes through 90° around one of its vertices.

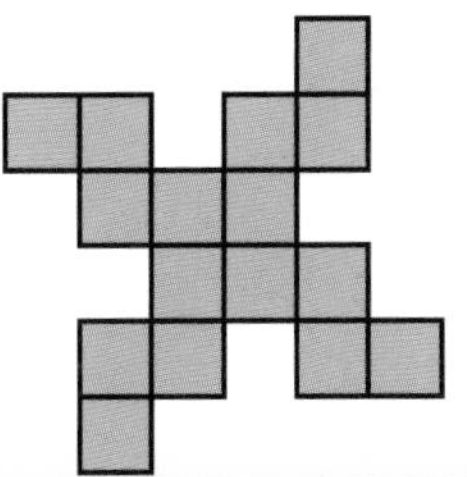

Which tetromino was used?

▲ **1** Make similar designs by rotating your tetrominoes around a dot on a piece of paper.

- Use any vertex as the centre of rotation.
- Rotate the shape through 90° clockwise or anticlockwise to make the design.

You need
cm squared paper or plain paper

■● **2** Rotate your tetrominoes on one of the coordinate grids on CM 19.

- Place one of the vertices on the origin and use this as the centre of rotation.
- Mark a cross on one of the vertices and follow this vertex as you rotate the shape.
- Rotate the shape through 90° clockwise three times.
- Record the coordinates of the vertex in each of the 4 positions.

You need
CM 19

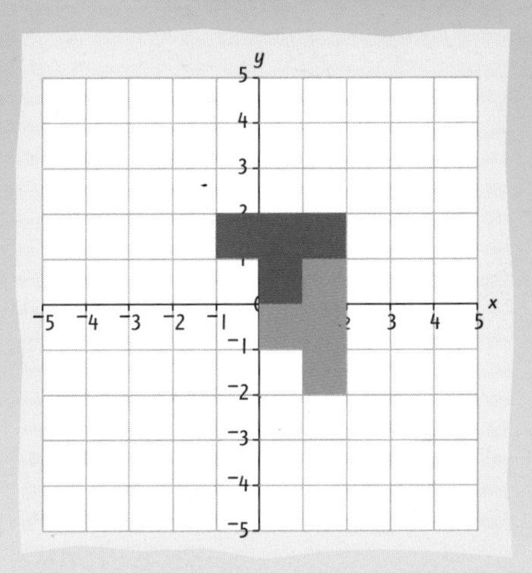

● **3** Repeat for pentominoes, made from 5 squares.

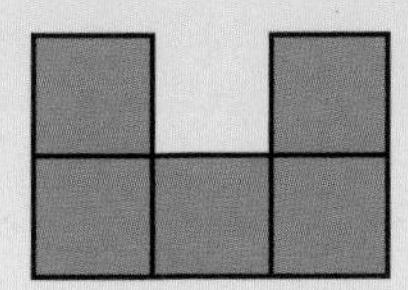

▲■● **1** Choose one of your tetromino shapes to place on a grid on CM 19.

You need
CM 19
tetromino shapes

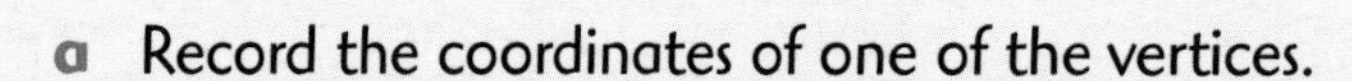

a Record the coordinates of one of the vertices.

b Reflect the shape first in the y-axis and then in the x-axis. Write the coordinates of the reflections of your chosen vertex.

c Repeat **a** and **b** with a different tetromino.

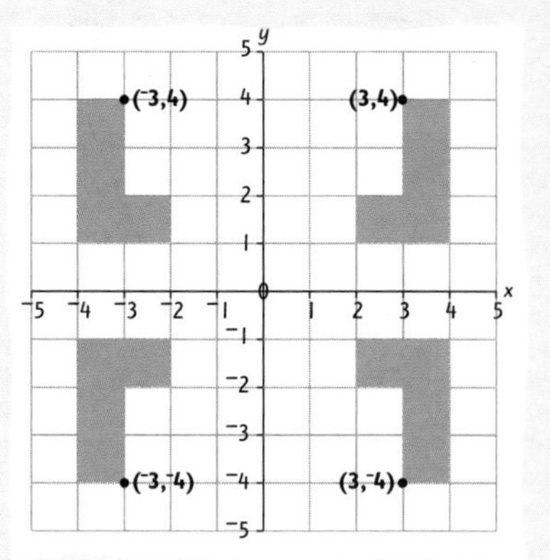

■ **2** These shapes have been reflected in both axes.
Write the coordinates of the vertices after each reflection.

a

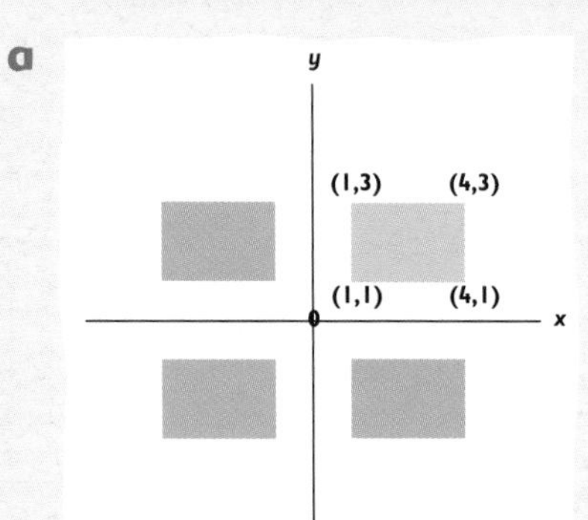

b

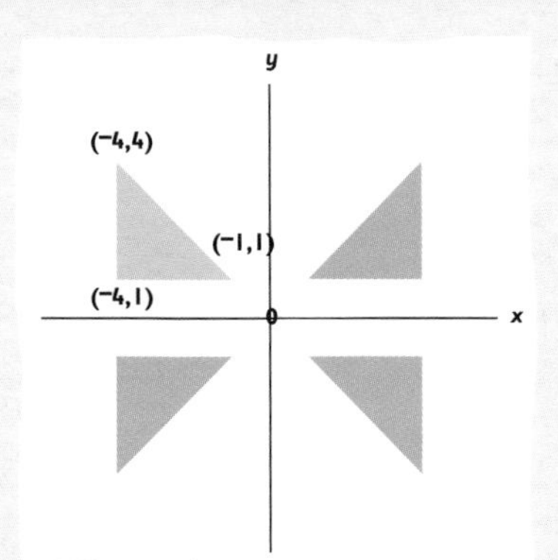

● **3** Imagine reflecting these shapes in both axes.

You need
plain paper
a ruler

a

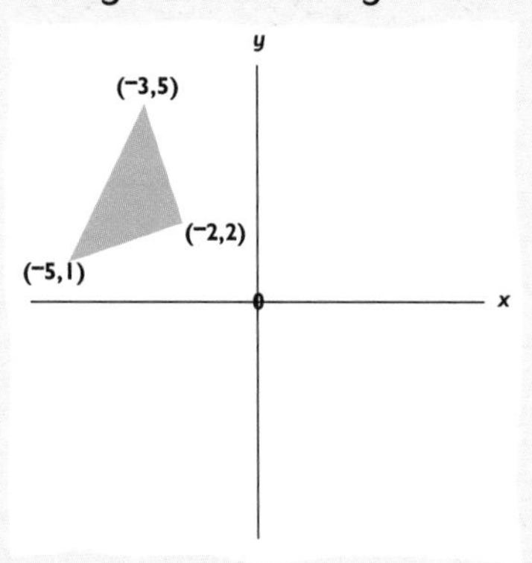

b

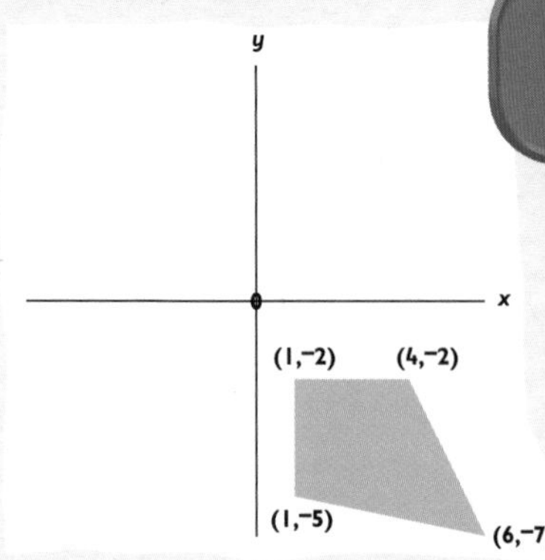

For each shape:

- Copy the shape and axes.
- Draw the reflections.
- Write the coordinates of the vertices of the reflected shapes.

▲■● **1** The table shows the distances thrown by some athletes in 3 throwing events at the 1996 Olympic Games.

Event	Weight	Athlete	Distance
Javelin	(m) 0·8 kg (f) 0·6 kg	J Zelezny P Felke	89·66 m 74·68 m
Discus	(m) 2 kg (f) 1 kg	L Riedel M Hellmann	69·40 m 83·22 m
Shot put	(m) 7·26 kg (f) 4 kg	U Timmermann I Slupianek	22·47 m 22·41 m

a How much further did Zelezny throw the javelin than Felke?

b How much shorter than Hellmann's discus throw was Reidel's?

c How much heavier is the shot that the men use than the one the women use?

d What was the difference between Slupianek's and Timmermann's distances in the shot put?

e How many grams heavier is the men's javelin than the women's?

■● **2a** What is the total distance of the men's throws in the 3 events?

b What is the total distance of the women's throws in the 3 events?

● **3a** Maria used the digits 1 to 9 in a rotating pattern to complete these 3 calculations:

9·87 + 6·54 − 3·21

1·98 + 7·65 − 4·32

2·19 + 8·76 − 5·43

Find the answers.

b Write the next 6 calculations in the pattern and find the answers.

1a Callum buys a football and a pair of football boots. What is the total cost?

b Nadia pays for a pair of cricket pads with a £50 note. How much change does she get?

c The coach at Tadcoster Cricket Club buys 4 boxes of cricket balls.
- How many cricket balls does he buy?
- What is the total cost?

d Hassan buys 13 football shirts for the school team. He gets a discount of £15·75. How much does he pay altogether?

2a A cricket ball is 7·85 cm in diameter. What are the minimum dimensions of a box of 6, arranged 3 by 2?

b Harry buys a baseball bat and a pair of trainers. He pays with two £20 notes. How much change will he get?

3a Lucy buys a pair of trainers and 2 cricket items. Altogether she pays £93·54. Which 2 cricket items did she buy?

b
- A golf ball is 4·28 cm in diameter. How many balls can a 17·3 cm × 21·6 cm × 8·8 cm box hold?
- The box costs £94. What is the price of one ball?

c Jim pays £242 for 8 golf clubs. Find the average cost of a club.

d Which 3 items would you like to buy? If you had two £50 notes, could you afford to buy them? How much change would you get?

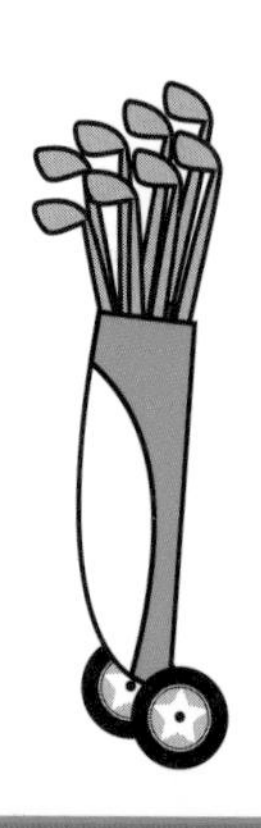

1 Brayshire played Donshire in a charity cricket match.

a 150 runs were scored altogether. Brayshire scored 10 more runs than Donshire. How many runs did each team score?

b Matt and Jed scored 22 runs between them. Matt scored 4 less than Jed. How many did each of them score?

c The 10 wickets for Donshire were taken by Rick and Dave. Dave took 2 more wickets than Dave. How many wickets did each of them take?

d During the Brayshire innings, £80 more was collected for charity than during the Donshire innings. Altogether £1120 was collected during the 2 innings. How much was collected during each innings?

2 In these questions, **A** and **B** represent numbers. Find what numbers **A** and **B** represent in each part.

a The sum of **A** and **B** is 36. The difference between **A** and **B** is 6.

b When **A** and **B** are added the answer is 6. When **B** is subtracted from **A** the answer is 1.

c **A** plus **B** is 7·3. **A** minus **B** is 2·1.

d **A** + **B** = 30 and **A** – **B** = ⁻2.

3 Each shape in this pair of calculations stands for a number.

Choose numbers from the pentagon and hexagon as the answers to the two calculations.

Find what numbers the square and triangle stand for.

Do this 5 times.

■ + ▲ = ⬟
■ – ▲ = ⬢

Pentagon: 10, 8·4, 3·78
Hexagon: 1·92, 16, 2·6

You need
CM 20

1 Each letter of the word MAGIC has 6 circles.

a Using CM 20, write the numbers 1, 2, 3, 4, 5 and 6 in the circles in the letter M, so that the sum of the numbers in each line is an odd number. Find different ways of doing it.

b Try to do the same for the letters A, G, I and C.

You need
a calculator

2 These calculations have something magical about them.

$(76{\cdot}2 + 87{\cdot}5) - (24{\cdot}9 + 38{\cdot}8)$

$(58{\cdot}21 + 79{\cdot}29) \div (5{\cdot}5 \times 0{\cdot}25)$

$(17{\cdot}31 - 11{\cdot}06) \times (9{\cdot}87 + 6{\cdot}13)$

Use a calculator to work out each answer.
Record the key presses you make each time.

What is magical about the calculations?

You will need to repeat some digits.

3 Copy and complete this blank magic calculation, using some or all of the digits 1 to 9.

(☐☐·☐☐ – ☐·☐) + (☐☐·☐ – ☐·☐☐) = 100

Unit 7 Use a calculator effectively. Check results with the inverse operation.
Check the sum of several numbers by adding in reverse order.
Confirm knowledge of sums and differences of odd and even numbers.

1 Estimate, then calculate, the size of each missing angle.

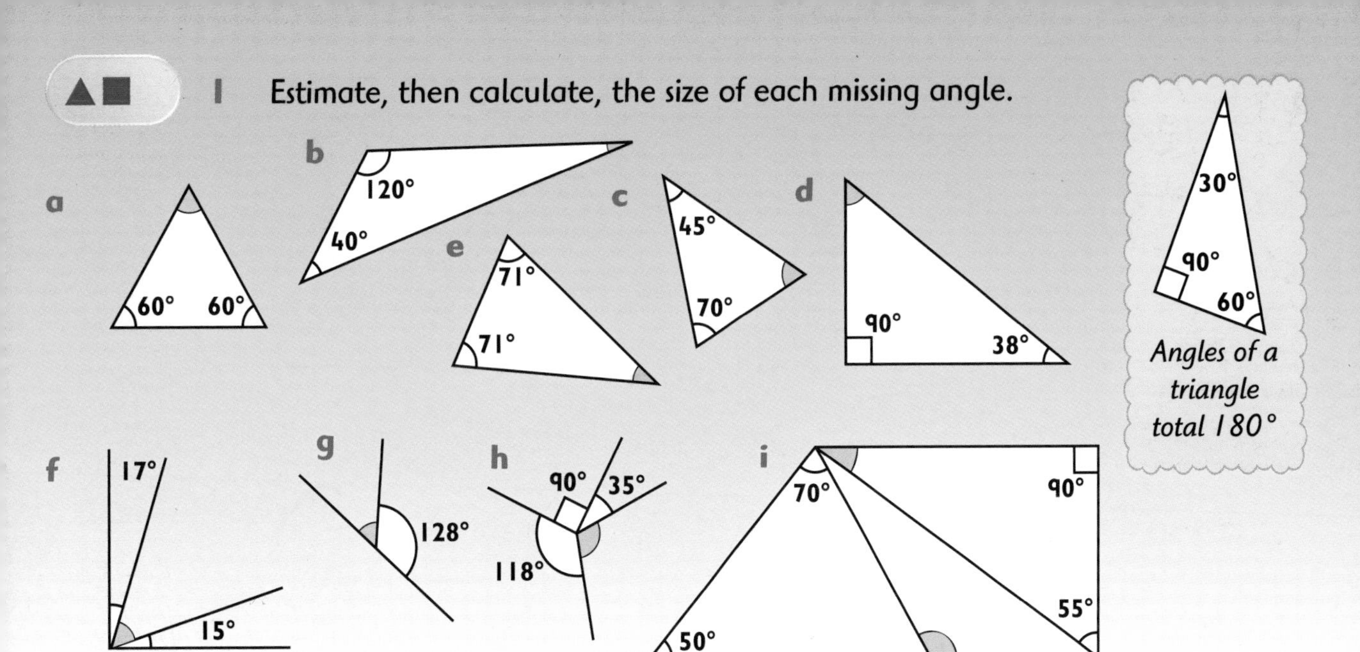

2 For each angle below:

- Draw a straight line, at least 12 cm long.
- Make a dot in the middle, draw and label the angle.
- Write the size of the other angle on the straight line.
- Label each of the angles *acute* or *obtuse*.

You need
a ruler
a protractor

a 25° b 63° c 95° d 124°

3a Draw a dot on a piece of paper.
Use shape tiles to find out which sets of shapes will fit exactly round this dot.

- Which sets of identical shapes will fit around the dot?
- How many equilateral triangles will fit around the dot?
- Which combinations of different quadrilaterals will fit around the dot?

You need
plain paper
shape tiles

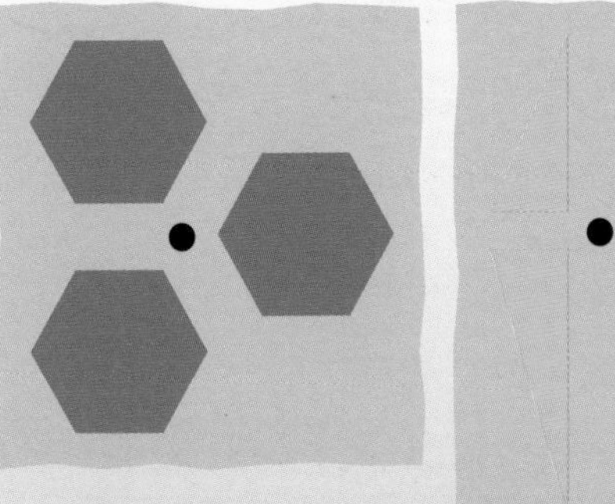

b What is the greatest number of shapes (identical or different) you can fit around the dot?

c What can you find out about the angles that meet at the dot?

You need interlocking shapes

1 Make this net of a cube using interlocking shapes.
Draw the net.

Make the cube, then carefully unfold it to make a different net.
Draw the new net.
Repeat for other nets of the cube.

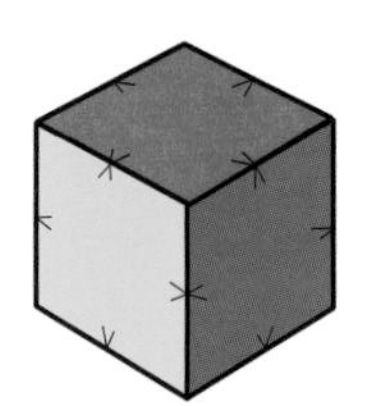

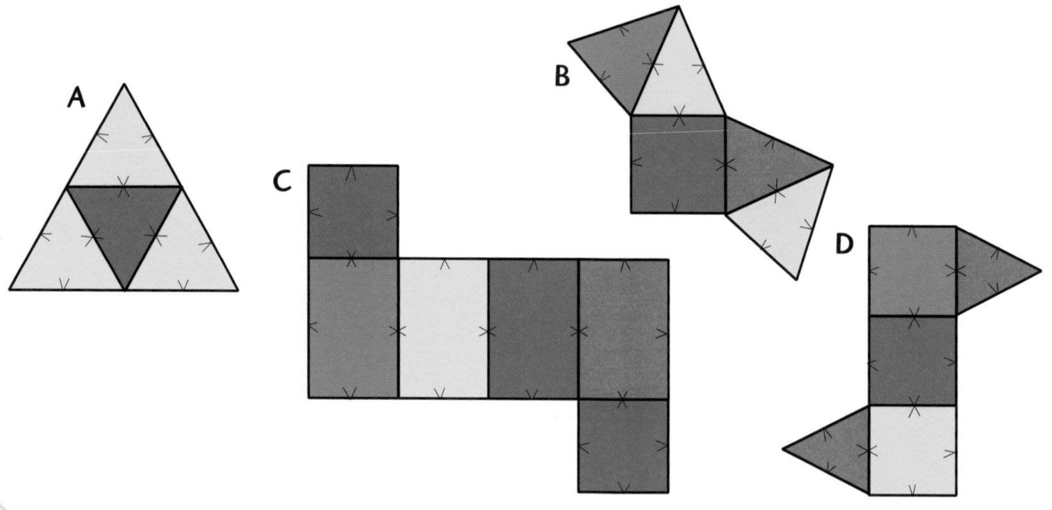

2 Try to predict the closed shapes of the nets **A** to **D**.
Check by making each shape.

3 Choose one of the nets **A** to **D** above.
Make the 3D shape and record the other nets that make it.

4 Choose one of the nets **A** to **D** above.
Without making the 3D shape, predict other nets that will make it.
Check your predictions by making the nets.

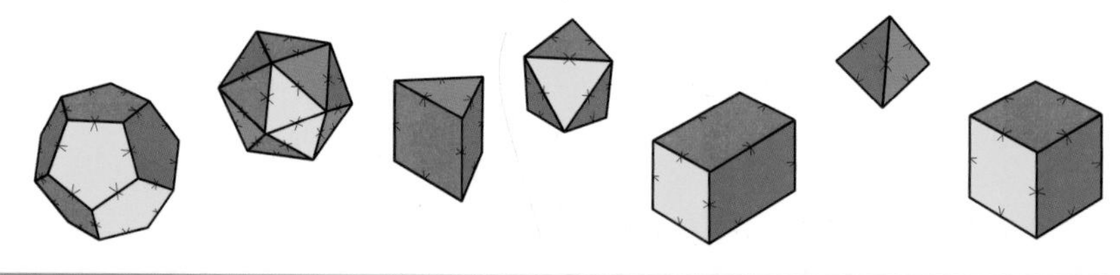

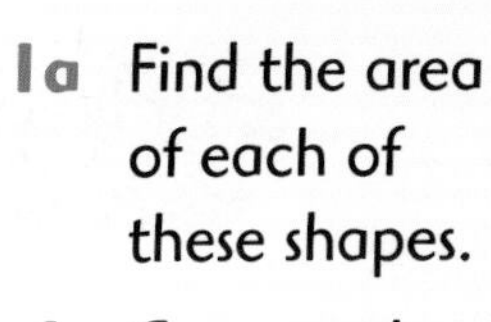

1a Find the area of each of these shapes.

b Copy each shape onto cm squared paper. Find the perimeter of each one.

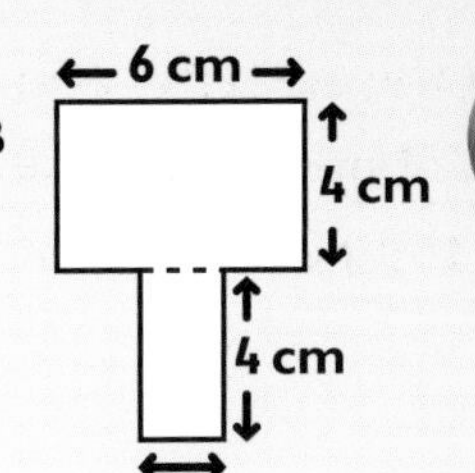

You need
cm squared paper

2 Two squares are joined to make each shape.
Find the missing length l in each shape.

a

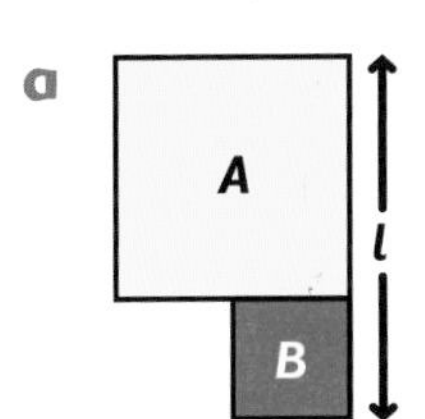

$A = 64\ \text{cm}^2$
$B = 16\ \text{cm}^2$
$l =$ ☐ cm

b

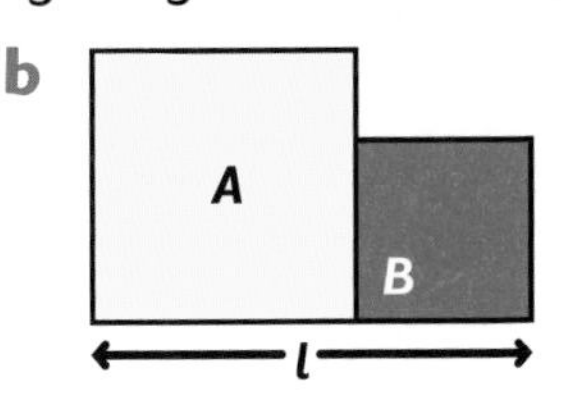

$A = 81\ \text{cm}^2$
$B = 36\ \text{cm}^2$
$l =$ ☐ cm

c

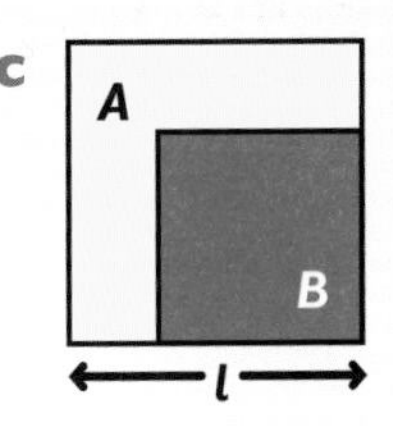

$A = 100\ \text{cm}^2$
$B = 49\ \text{cm}^2$
$l =$ ☐ cm

d

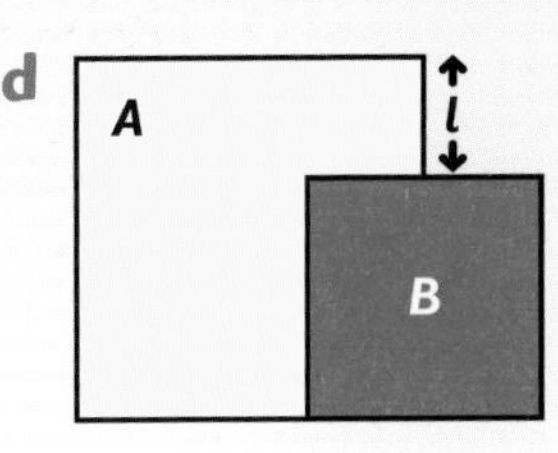

$A = 144\ \text{cm}^2$
$B = 64\ \text{cm}^2$
$l =$ ☐ cm

3 A square is joined to a rectangle to make an L shape.
The L shape has an area of $36\ \text{cm}^2$.

Find the longest and shortest perimeter of the L shape when the square has an area of:

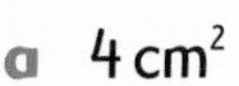

a $4\ \text{cm}^2$ **b** $9\ \text{cm}^2$ **c** $16\ \text{cm}^2$ **d** $25\ \text{cm}^2$

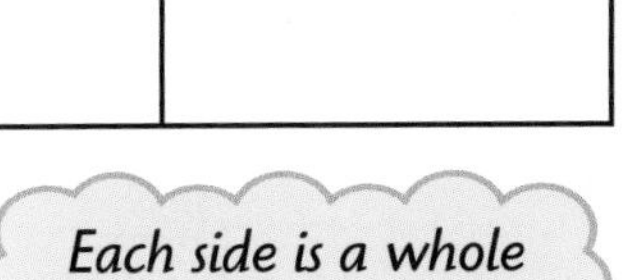

4 Two rectangles are joined to make an L shape.

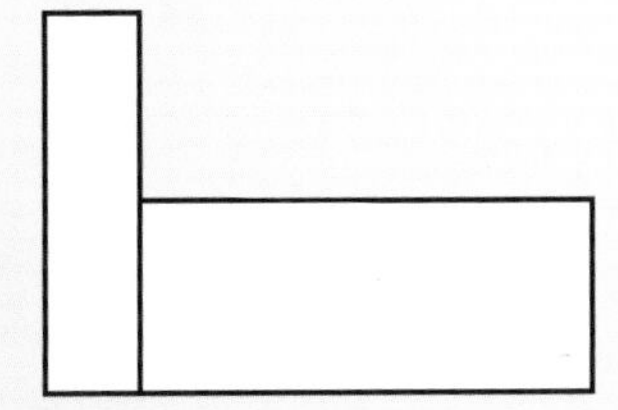

Investigate the longest perimeter of the L shape when the combined area of the rectangles is $36\ \text{cm}^2$.

Write about what you notice.

$(1 + 35)\ \text{cm}^2$
$(2 + 34)\ \text{cm}^2$
$(3 + 33)\ \text{cm}^2$
⋮
$(18 + 18)\ \text{cm}^2$
Each side is a whole number of centimetres.

1 Choose the best estimate for each measurement.

a 

2 feet   2 m   2 miles

b 

0·1 km   1000 m   1 mile

c 

70 lb   70 t   700 kg

d 

200 g   20 oz   2 lb

e 

$\frac{1}{2}$ lb   1 kg   150 g

f 

3 l   33 cl   3 pints

2 Write 2 things that could be measured in:

a ounces   b miles   c pints   d yards.

3 How could you measure each of these, and what units could you use?

a the mass of a dog   b the length of a car   c the capacity of a water bottle

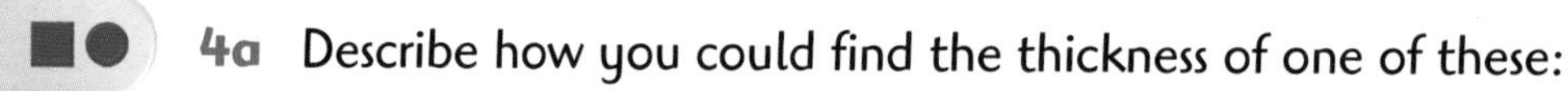

4a Describe how you could find the thickness of one of these:
- a piece of string
- a playing card
- a 2p coin.

b Describe how you could find the mass of one of these:
- a paper clip
- a marble
- a plastic pen cap.

5 This carton holds 1 litre of orange juice. Another carton is twice the height, length and width of this carton. How many litres does it hold?

6 This table gives the mass of each newspaper.
Sort the papers so that 3 children each deliver:
- 20 newspapers
- at least one copy of each newspaper
- a total mass greater than 5 kg and less than 6 kg
- a different set of newspapers from each other.

Newspaper	Mass
Mail	230 g
Record	200 g
Post	120 g
Herald	300 g
Times	500 g
Express	320 g

1 Copy and complete.

a $0{\cdot}6\,kg = 250\,g + \square\,g$

b $2\,l - 750\,ml = \square\,l$

c $0{\cdot}85\,kg = 1200\,g - \square\,g$

d $470\,ml + \square\,cl = 0{\cdot}9\,l$

e $3{\cdot}125\,kg = \square\,g + 0{\cdot}65\,kg$

f $\square\,l - 2{\cdot}05\,l = 1700\,ml$

2 Which is the better buy for each of these items, the special offer or the shelf price?

		Special offer	Shelf price
a	Shampoo	2 × 300 ml for £3	200 ml for £1·10
b	Cola	12 × 15 cl cans for £3·60	2 × 1 l bottles for £2·90
c	Bacon	250 g for £2·25	200 g for £1·84
d	Cornflakes	$\frac{3}{4}$ kg for £1·39	500 g for 95p

3a Find the lowest and the greatest possible mass for 6 eggs that are:

- medium
- large.

small	medium	large	very large
under 53 g	53 g–62 g	63 g–72 g	73 g or more

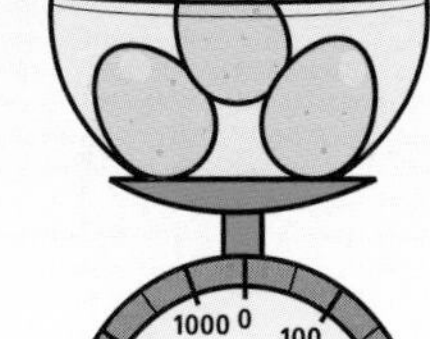
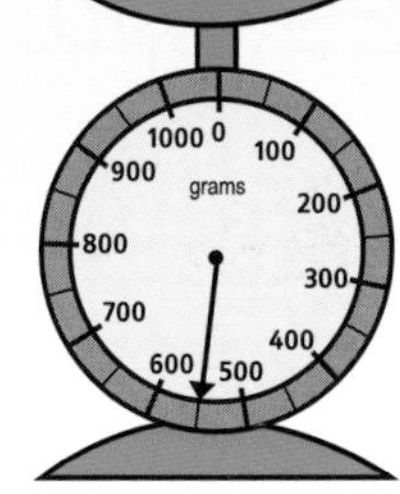

b Jamie used 3 eggs of the same size to make scrambled eggs. His empty bowl weighed 350 g. Find the size of egg he used.

c The average mass of 6 large eggs is 400 g. About how many large eggs are there in 1 kg?

4 At the start of a competition, 5 athletes have identical, full bottles of water. At the end, each bottle has some water left.

- Cody's bottle does not hold the least, and Owen's does not hold the most.
- Owen's bottle has more than Ella's.
- Ben's bottle has more than Cody's.
- Only one bottle has less than Danny's.
- 2 bottles are fuller than Cody's.

a List the 5 bottles in order of the amount of water left, most water first.

b The amounts of water left in the bottles are:

55 ml   0·5 l   15 cl $\frac{1}{4}$ l   100 ml

How much water does each athlete have left?

1a Complete the conversion scale on CM 21 for **ounces and grams** up to 1000 g.

You need
CM 21

b Use the scale to find the number of grams, to the nearest 10 g, for each of these:

Honey 24oz

2 Use the **ounces and grams** scale on CM 21 to convert these masses:

a 16 oz, 10 oz, 21 oz, 3 oz, 29 oz

b 90 g, 600 g, 510 g, 250 g, 480 g

Round your answers to the nearest whole ounce or 10 g.

3a Complete the conversion scale on CM 21 for **miles and kilometres.**

b Find each distance in kilometres.

Town	Distance from Glasgow (miles)
Edinburgh	45
Oban	90
Gourock	25
Ayr	33
Perth	57
Hamilton	11

4a Complete the conversion scale on CM 21 for **gallons and litres.**

b Find the fuel tank capacity in litres, to the nearest litre, for each boat.

Boat	Fuel tank capacity
Puffin	5·8 gallons
Mallard	8·8 gallons
Sandpiper	6·7 gallons
Seahawk	4·5 gallons
Kittiwake	7·3 gallons

5a Copy and complete the table.
Round your answers to the nearest pound.

You need
a calculator

Young seal	A	B	C	D	E	F	G
Mass in kg	20	26	29	35	47	56	64
Mass in lb							

1 kg ≈ 2·2 lb

14 lb = 1 stone

b Write each seal's mass in stones and pounds.

1 Find the cost of:

Cheddar	500 g	100 g	600 g
Ham	100 g	50 g	250 g
Paté	200 g	20 g	180 g
Olives	100 g	1000 g	800 g
Salmon	100 g	500 g	150 g

2 The lid of a rectangular box is twice as long as it is wide. The sum of the length and the width is 87mm. What does the lid measure in centimetres?

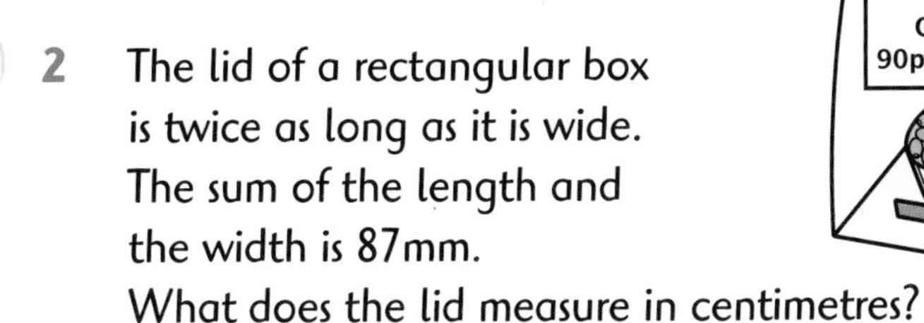

3 A carton of orange and a slice of pizza costs £1·70. A carton of orange and 2 slices of pizza costs £2·65. Find the cost of:

a one slice of pizza **b** one carton of orange.

4 Sheena knitted a blue and white blanket. She used an exact number of balls of wool.

a How many balls of each colour were needed, if she used a total of 800 g of wool?

b How much did the blanket cost to knit?

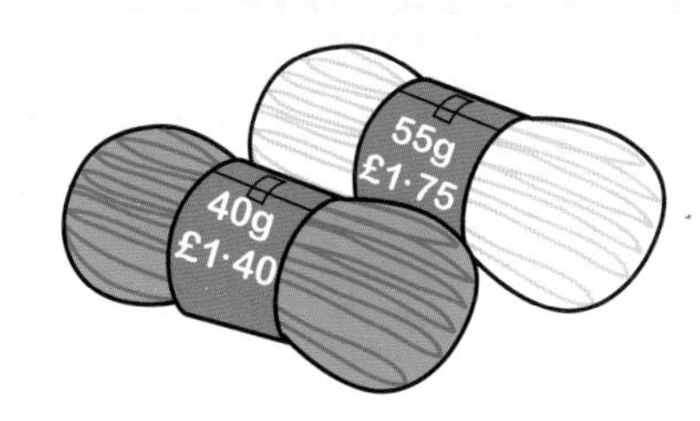

5 Jake uses 60 cm × 30 cm slabs to make a path 60 cm wide.

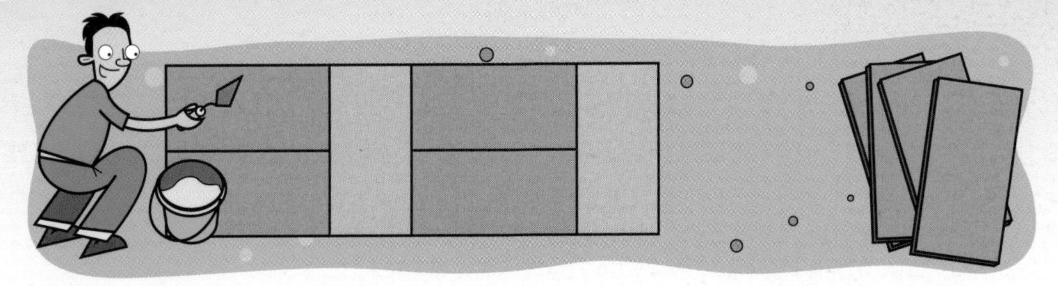

a Find how many different arrangements he can make with 6 slabs.

b Jake leaves 5 mm gaps between the slabs. Find the length of:

- the shortest path
- the longest path.

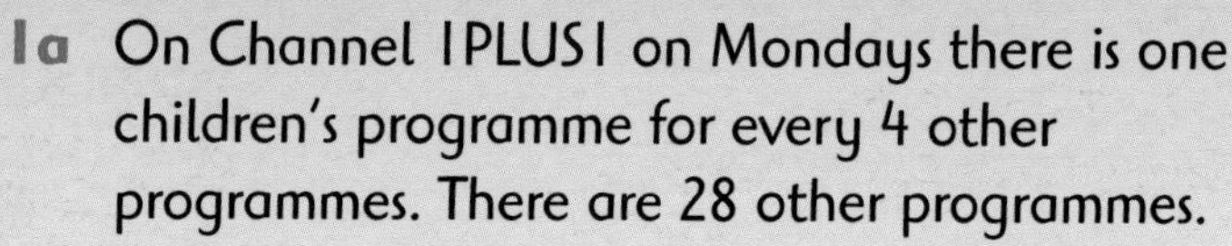

1a On Channel 1PLUS1 on Mondays there is one children's programme for every 4 other programmes. There are 28 other programmes.

- Draw a number line and count up to find the number of children's programmes.

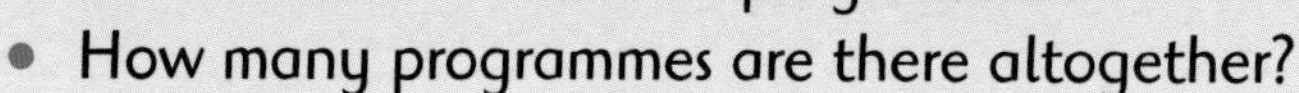

- How many programmes are there altogether?

children's programmes
1 2 3
4 8
other programmes

b On Tuesdays, the total number of programmes is the same, but there are 2 children's programmes for every 5 other programmes. How many children's programmes are there?

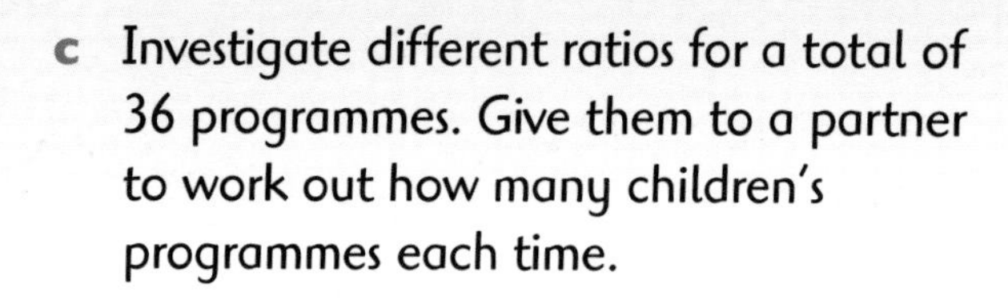

c Investigate different ratios for a total of 36 programmes. Give them to a partner to work out how many children's programmes each time.

For example: 1 children's programme for every 5 other programmes gives 6 children's programmes.

2 There are 14 children's programmes on Channel 2PLUS2 each weekday.

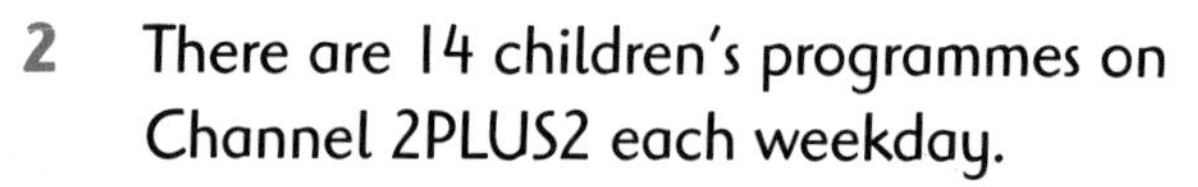

a Look at the diagram showing the kinds of children's programmes each day.

- What is the proportion of dramas?
- How many dramas each day?

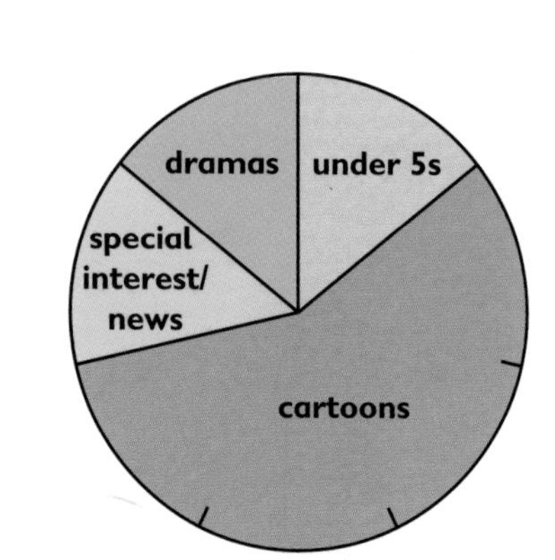

b Draw a number line and count up to find the number of dramas and the total number of children's programmes from Monday to Friday.

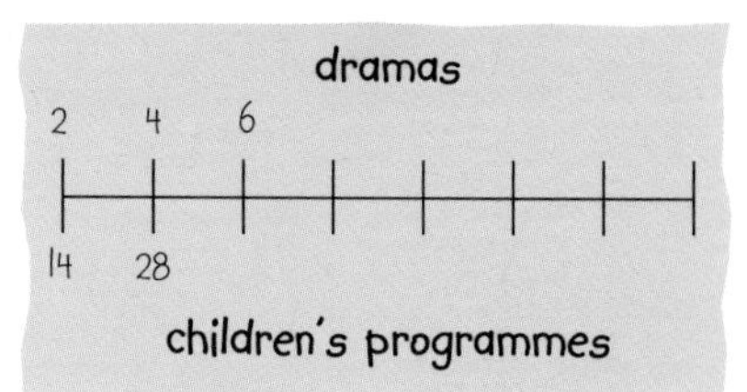

c Repeat **a** and **b** for cartoons.

3 Work in a group.

- Look at the listings for television programmes for one weekday. Each choose a channel.
- Work out how much time is given to these different types of programme between 6.00 am and 6.00 pm on different channels.

You need
television programme listings

Children's | **Soaps/dramas/films** | **Home and garden**

Travel | **News** | **Other (chat programmes, game shows...)**

- Find the approximate proportion for each type of programme.

1a Copy and complete the table.

euros	1	5	10	15	20
pence	70	350			
£	0·70				

You need
CM 22
a ruler

Use the ratio: about 1 euro for every 70p.

b Use the table to plot pounds against euros on CM 22. Use a ruler to join the points.

c Look at each small square on the axis for euros. What does it represent?

d Find about how many:

- euros for £1, £5, £10, £12·50
- pounds for €9, €12, €17.

1 euro = 100 cents

Round your answers to the nearest 50 cents or 50p.

2a Work with a partner.
Discuss how to draw accurate graphs, based on current exchange rates, for converting up to £10 to euros and to American dollars.
Talk about:

- where to find the exchange rates
- different graph papers and the scales to use.

You need
a calculator
graph paper
a ruler

b Each draw one conversion graph carefully.

c Swap graphs and find pound equivalents for these euro and dollar prices:

3a Work with a partner.
Try to use your graphs from question 2 to draw a graph to convert euros to dollars.

b Try it on the euro prices in question 2.

c How do the French prices in euros for soft toys compare with the American prices in dollars?

A dentist carried out a survey among her patients. She asked:

- *Do you eat chocolate nearly every day?*
- *Do you eat other kinds of sweets nearly every day?*

She noted the age group of everyone who replied *Yes* to either question.

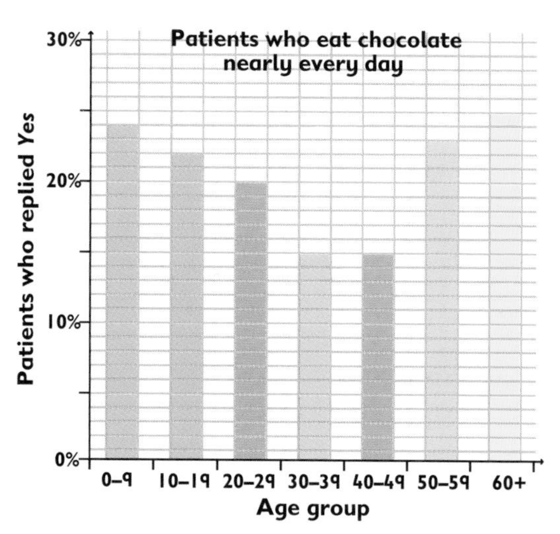

1 The bar chart above shows the percentage of patients in each age group who replied *Yes* to the dentist's first question.

a Copy and complete the table.

Age group	0–9	10–19	20–29	30–39	40–49	50–59	60+
Percentage who eat chocolate nearly every day							

b In the 10–19 age group, what percentage replied *No*?

c In which age group did 77% of the people reply *No*?

d If there were 56 people in the 60+ age group, how many replied *Yes*?

2 This table shows the percentage of patients who replied *Yes* to the dentist's second question.

Age group	0–9	10–19	20–29	30–39	40–49	50–59	60+
Percentage who eat sweets nearly every day	29%	27%	19%	10%	12%	20%	21%

a Draw a bar chart to show this information.

b Use the information to write 3 statements about the dentist's patients.

c Write 2 sensible questions about patients and sweets that the dentist cannot answer from the table or graph.

3 Carry out a survey in your own age group. Compare your findings with those of the dentist. Do you think all the patients who replied *No* were telling the truth?

1 The pie charts show children's favourite activities at the winter sports holiday centre.

You need
CM 23

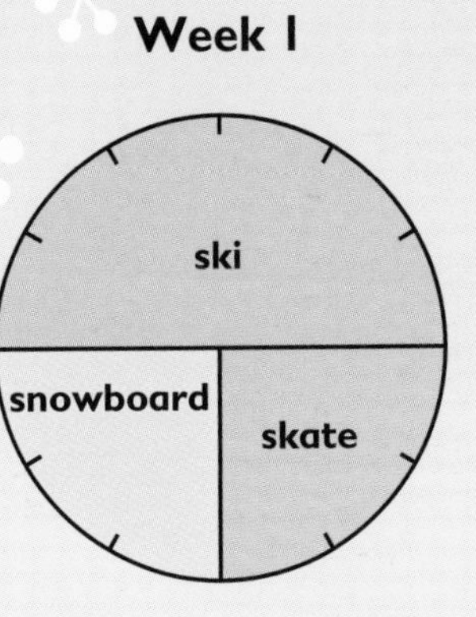

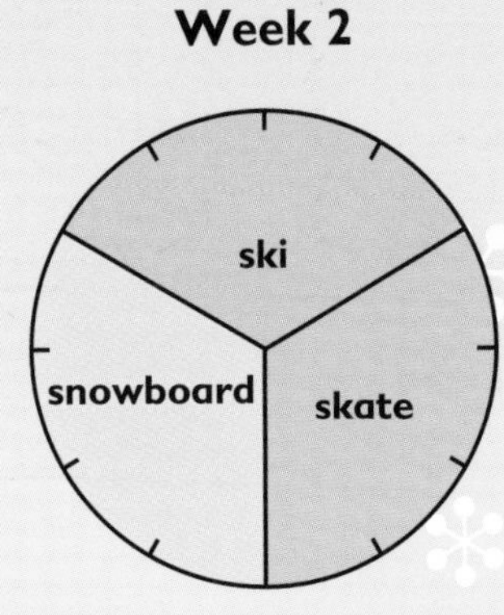

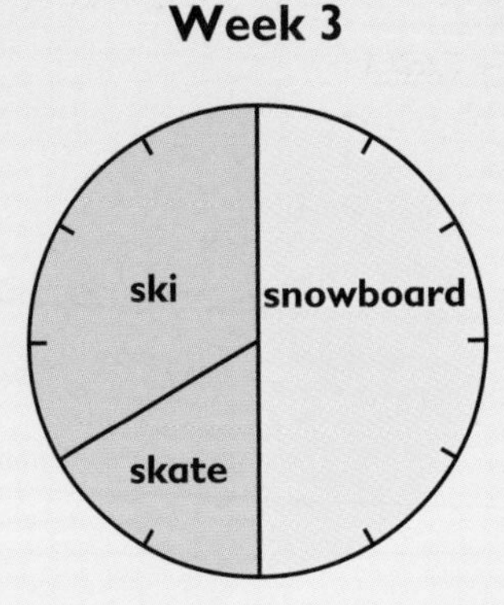

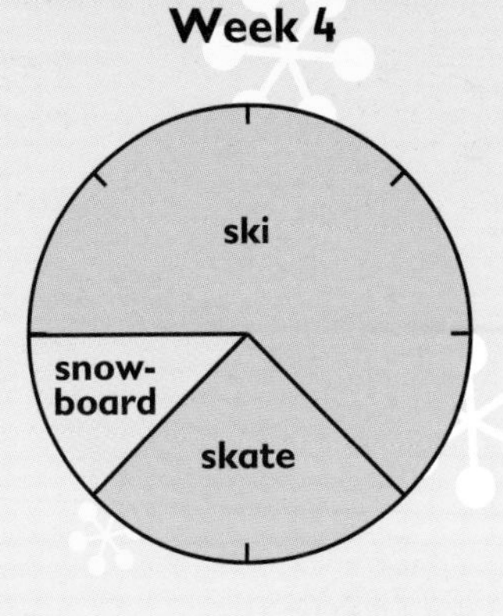

Use the pie charts to complete the **database** on CM 23.

2a Use your database to find in which weeks:

You need
a ruler

- equal numbers chose skiing, snowboarding and skating as their favourite
- twice as many chose skating as chose snowboarding
- $\frac{5}{8}$ of the children liked skiing best
- half chose skiing as their favourite and equal numbers chose snowboarding and skating.

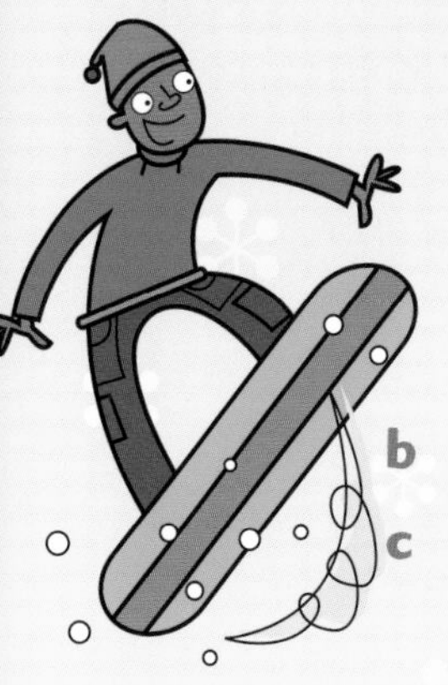

b How many more children liked skating best in week 4 than in week 1?

c Complete the pie charts on CM 23 to show the information in this table:

Week	Total number of children	Number who preferred ...			
		skiing	snowboarding	skating	sledging
5	36	18	9	6	3
6	48	28	12	4	4

3a Write 3 statements describing how the pie charts for weeks 5 and 6 are similar or different.

b If, in week 6, 24 children had chosen skiing as their favourite and 8 had chosen skating, how would the pie chart be different?

1 Parminder goes horse-riding each Saturday. She has a lesson every 3 weeks and a competition every 4 weeks. How often does she have a lesson and a competition on the same day?

2a Find the numbers in this grid that are multiples of 4.

S 27	G 31	F 35	L 8	I 40	L 9	C 7	B 4	D 36
F 70	E 54	N 24	I 49	R 21	E 18	U 12	D 42	A 14

Write the matching letters.
Rearrange the letters to make the name of a city.

b Repeat for multiples of 6, 7 and 9.

All the cities are in Britain or Ireland.

3 Write 4 numbers that would fit in the green part of each Venn diagram.

a

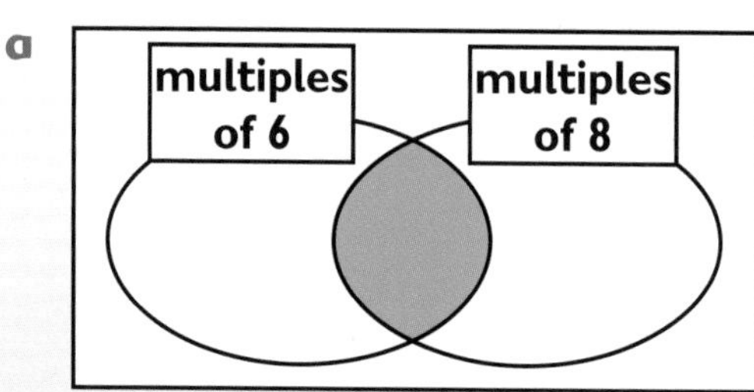

b

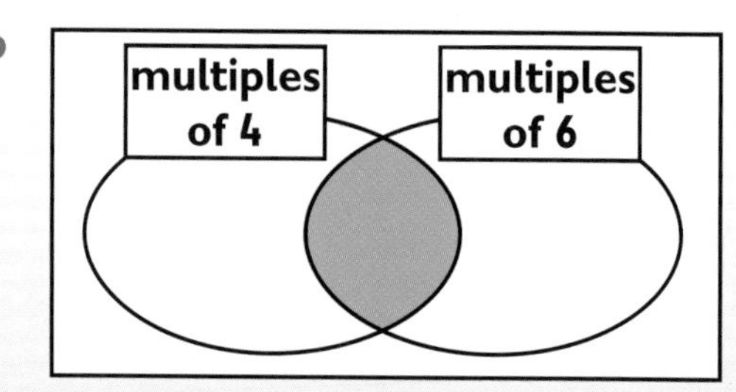

c

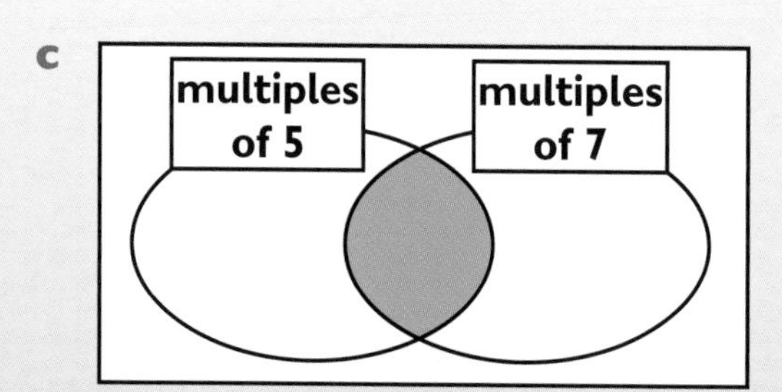

d

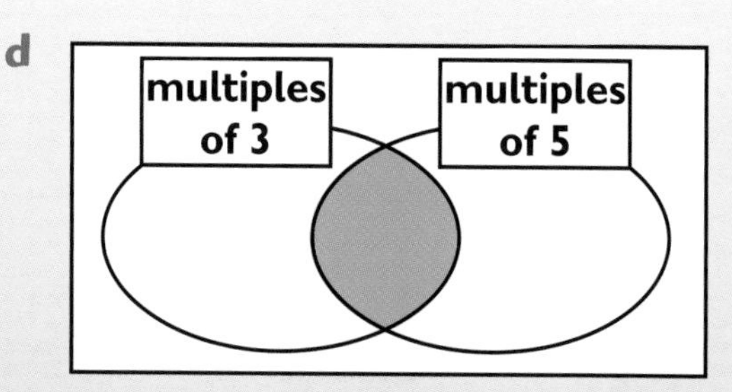

4 What are the lowest common multiples for each pair of numbers in question 3?

Three in a Line is a game for 2 players. The aim is to get 3 of your counters in a line in any of these directions:

You need
CM 24
a blank dice
32 coloured counters each

Take turns to:
- roll the dice
- choose a number on the gameboard on CM 24 that is divisible by the dice number
- place one of your counters on the number.

The player who is the first to get 3 counters in a line wins.

▲ 1 Write the numbers 2, 3 and 5 on your dice, each one twice.

■ 2 Write the numbers 4, 5 and 6 on your dice, each one twice.

● 3 Write the numbers 6, 8 and 9 on your dice, each one twice.

▲■● 4 What if you changed the rules? For example:

Make it a 'four in a line' game.

Roll 2 dice. Choose a number that is divisible by both dice numbers.

1 Which of the numbers on the leaves are:

a prime numbers?

b multiples of 3?

c factors of 45?

d prime factors of 30?

A prime number is only divisible by 1 and itself. It has exactly 2 factors. Prime factors are factors that are also prime numbers.

The factors of 15 are 1, 3, 5 and 15. The prime factors of 15 are 3 and 5.

2 One way of working out prime factors is to use factor trees. For example:

Start with any pair of factors of 36 and factorise them. Continue until you get prime factors.

$3 \times 2 \times 2 \times 3 = 36$

2 and 3 are prime factors of 36

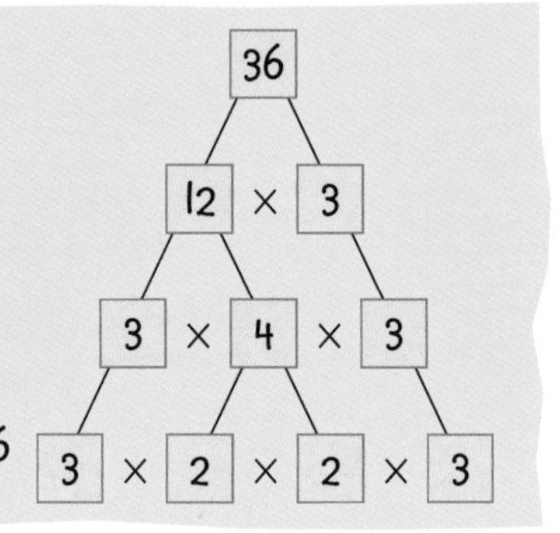

Copy and complete these factor trees:

a

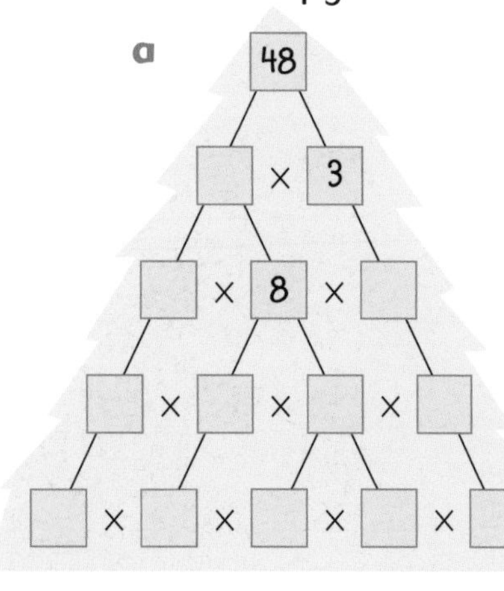

b

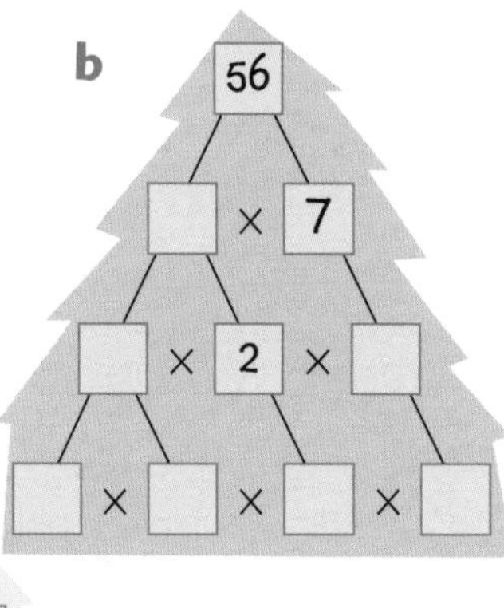

c

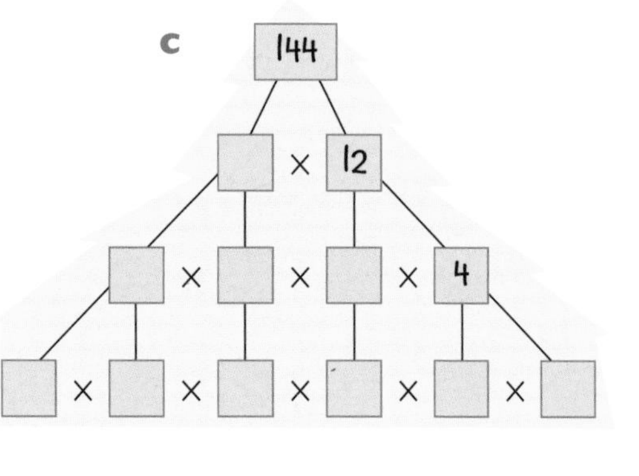

3 Make factor trees to find the prime factors of these numbers:

a 42

b 90

c 72

d 132

▲■● 1 On your pieces of paper write the numbers:

▲ 1 to 25 ■ 1 to 20 ● 1 to 16

Place the pieces of paper on the grid so that they follow the rules. Copy the completed grid.

You need
small pieces of paper
25 each for ▲
20 each for ■
16 each for ●

	<12	square number	multiple of 3	>6
odd number				
factor of 24				
<8				
even number				

Work out the missing digits in questions **2** to **4**.

▲ **2a** ☐7 × ☐ = 81

b 4☐ × ☐2 = 990

c 3☐ × 1☐ = 476

You can check with a calculator.

You need
a calculator

■ **3a** 6☐ × ☐8 = 1820

b 1☐4 × 3☐ = 5248

c ☐☐3 × 4☐ = 6435

● **4a** ☐4 × 8☐ = 2822

b ☐☐2 × 5☐ = 10 738

c 54 × 7☐ = 4☐☐4

1a Roll all the dice.
Arrange them in different ways to make 6 different numbers. Use at least 2 digits each time.
Record all your numbers.

b Write the numbers in order, from smallest to largest.

c Repeat parts **a** and **b** twice.

You need
3 dice

Make whole numbers and numbers with decimal places.

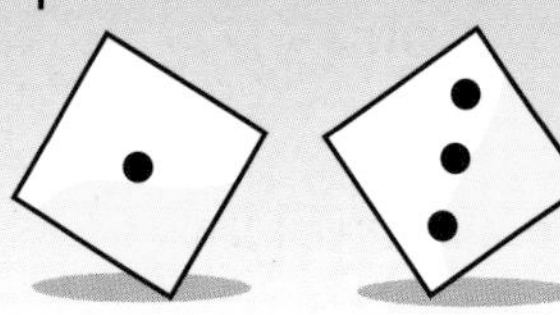

1.34
3.41
4.1

2a Play **Round to Win** with a partner.

- Each draw a 2 by 3 grid. Write in 6 different whole numbers between 1 and 7.
- Take turns to roll all the dice. Arrange 2 of the digits to make a number with 1 decimal place.
- Round the number you have made to the nearest whole number.
- If that number appears on your grid, cross it off.
- Check your partner's answers.

The winner is the first person to cross off all their numbers.

b Play again, but this time use your dice scores to make numbers with 2 decimal places.

You need
3 dice per pair

8	7
1	4
6	2

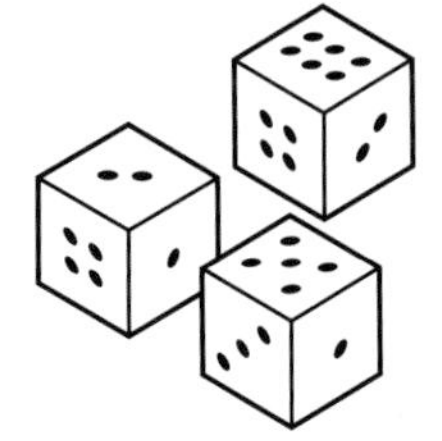

3a Play **Round to Win** with a partner.

- Each draw a 2 by 3 grid. Write in 6 different whole numbers between 0 and 20.
- Take turns to roll all the dice. Arrange the digits to make a number with 2 or 3 decimal places.
- Round the number you have made to the nearest whole number.
- If that number appears on your grid, cross it off.
- Check your partner's answers.

The winner is the first person to cross off all their numbers.

b Play again, but this time write in grid numbers between 0 and 20 with 1 decimal place.
Round the numbers you make to the nearest tenth.

You need
4 dice per pair, including at least one 0–9

You need
CM 25

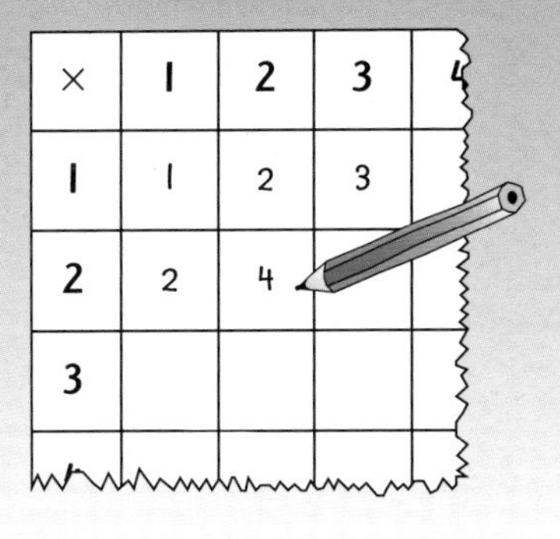

▲

1a Complete the multiplication grid on CM 25.
Use it to answer parts **b**, **c** and **d**.

b Find 3 fractions equivalent to:

- $\frac{2}{3}$
- $\frac{3}{4}$
- $\frac{3}{5}$
- $\frac{2}{6}$

c Use the grid to find each missing number:

- $\frac{1}{2} = \frac{6}{\square}$
- $\frac{1}{5} = \frac{\square}{20}$
- $\frac{5}{6} = \frac{\square}{18}$
- $\frac{\square}{4} = \frac{9}{12}$

d Find the simplest equivalent fraction for:

- $\frac{2}{4}$
- $\frac{2}{10}$
- $\frac{5}{15}$
- $\frac{4}{6}$

e Explain how you found the simplest equivalent fraction for $\frac{4}{6}$.

■

2a Make a list of all the proper fractions with the denominator 8.
Cancel them until each one is in its lowest terms.

b Explain how you know they are all in their lowest terms.

3a Investigate more sets of proper fractions with denominators 7, 9, 10, 11 and 12.

b Which sets have no fractions that can be cancelled?
What do you notice about their denominators?

●

4a Sandeep cancelled $\frac{12}{48}$ like this:

$$\frac{12}{48} = \frac{6}{24} = \frac{3}{12} = \frac{1}{4}$$

Describe how he could have done it in one step.

The highest common factor of two whole numbers is the greatest whole number that divides into both exactly.

b Use the highest common factor to cancel each fraction to its lowest terms.

- $\frac{20}{50}$
- $\frac{18}{24}$
- $\frac{27}{45}$
- $\frac{21}{84}$

c Sandeep noticed that $\frac{21}{84} = \frac{12}{48}$.

- What is special about this pair of fractions?
- Investigate other pairs of equivalent fractions where the 2 digits of the denominator and the numerator have been reversed.
- What if the denominator and the numerator both had 3 digits?

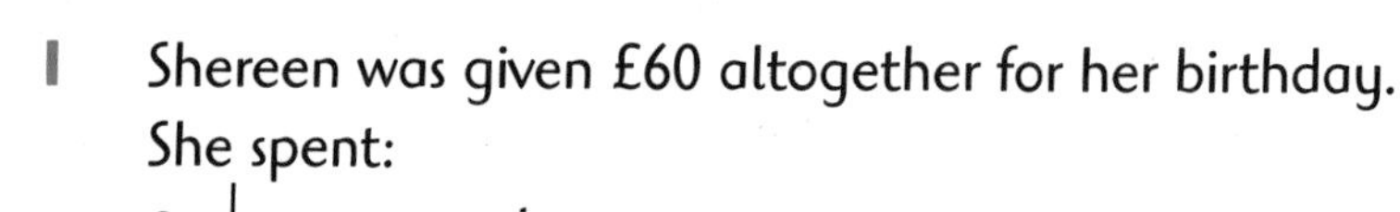

1 Shereen was given £60 altogether for her birthday.
She spent:

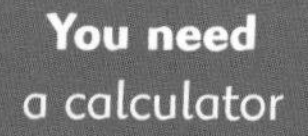

- $\frac{1}{2}$ on computer games
- $\frac{1}{3}$ of what was left after the games on a netball
- $\frac{1}{4}$ of what was left after the netball on a book
- $\frac{1}{5}$ of what was left after the book on a pen
- $\frac{1}{6}$ of what was left after the pen on a magazine
- $\frac{2}{5}$ of what was left after the magazine on a hat
- $\frac{3}{4}$ of what was left after the hat on a video
- $\frac{2}{3}$ of what was left after the video on a notebook.

Work out how much money she had left.

2a Write which envelope contains more money:

You need
a calculator

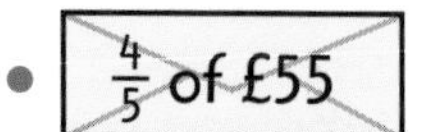

- $\frac{4}{5}$ of £55 or $\frac{2}{3}$ of £60?
- $\frac{5}{6}$ of £120 or $\frac{3}{4}$ of £160?
- $\frac{1}{3}$ of £177 or $\frac{1}{7}$ of £434?

b Write which distance is longer:

- $\frac{1}{3}$ of 495 m or $\frac{3}{8}$ of 400 m?
- $\frac{4}{7}$ of 28 miles or $\frac{1}{4}$ of 56 miles?
- $\frac{1}{3}$ of 870 m or $\frac{3}{10}$ of 1 km?

c Explain how you chose your answers in parts **a** and **b**.

3a Copy and complete each calculation.
Write one digit for each □.

You need
digit cards 0–9

$\frac{□}{□}$ of □ kg = 3500 g

$\frac{□}{□}$ of □ m = 40 cm

$\frac{□}{□}$ of £□□ = £20

b Repeat part **a**, but this time use each digit from 0 to 9 once only.
Use digit cards to try out possible solutions. Record your trials.

4 Look at question 1. Make up a similar problem for your partner to solve.

*Try starting with the answer.
Use inverse operations to work back to the start number or quantity.*

1 Look at CM 26. The clouds show ways of finding different percentages.

You need
CM 26
a calculator

a Draw a line to match each cloud to a suitable calculation further down the sheet.

b Choose 6 calculations from the boxes and work out the answers without a calculator.
Show your method. Include any jottings.

c Use a calculator to check your answers.

d Use a calculator to do the rest of the calculations.

Divide by 100 to find 1%, then multiply.

2a Look at the **strategies** and **calculations** on CM 26. Choose 6 calculations from the boxes and work out the answers without a calculator. Show your method.

You need
CM 26
a calculator

b Explain why you chose these 6 calculations.

c Use a calculator to do the rest of the calculations.

3 52% of this rectangle is blue.
What area of the rectangle is blue?
Show your method.

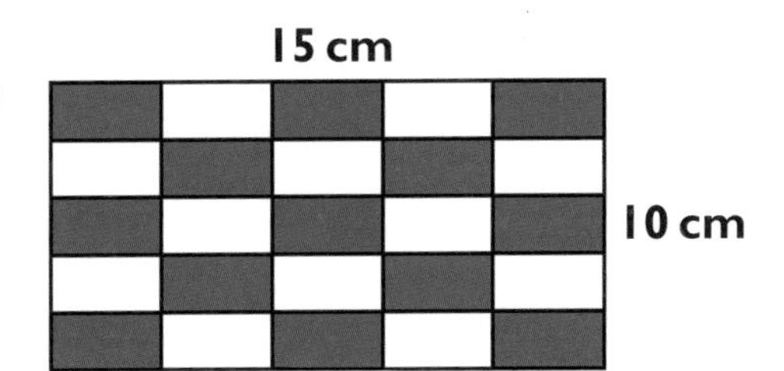

4

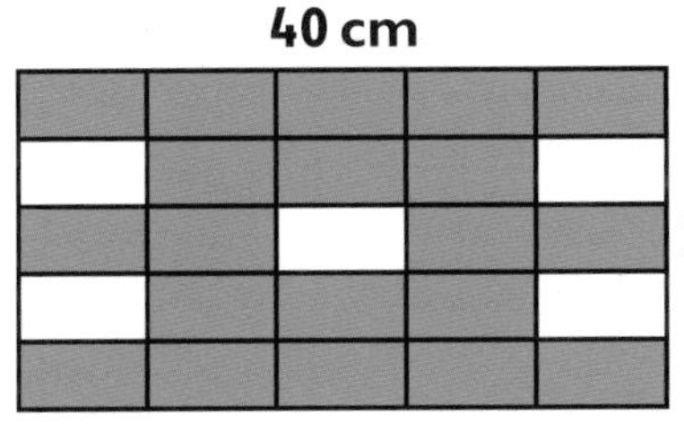

a What percentage of the rectangle above is red?

b What area of the rectangle is red?

c What area of the rectangle is white?

1a Class 6 practise for the school sponsored walk. They walk 718 m across one field and then 575 m across another. How far do they walk altogether?

b Their second practice is in the country. They walk 2·93 km, stop for some water and then walk another 1·87 km. What is the total distance they walk?

c Their last practice walk is 5326 m long. After 3281 m they stop for lunch. How much further do they still have to walk?

d The sponsored walk is 8·52 km, with a break after 4·87 km. What distance is there still to walk after the break?

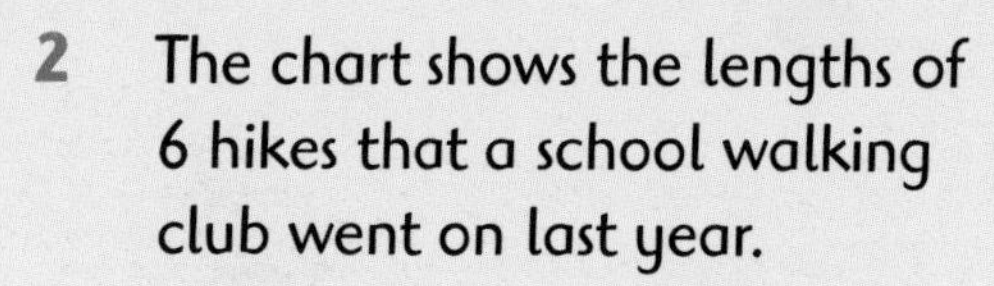

2 The chart shows the lengths of 6 hikes that a school walking club went on last year.

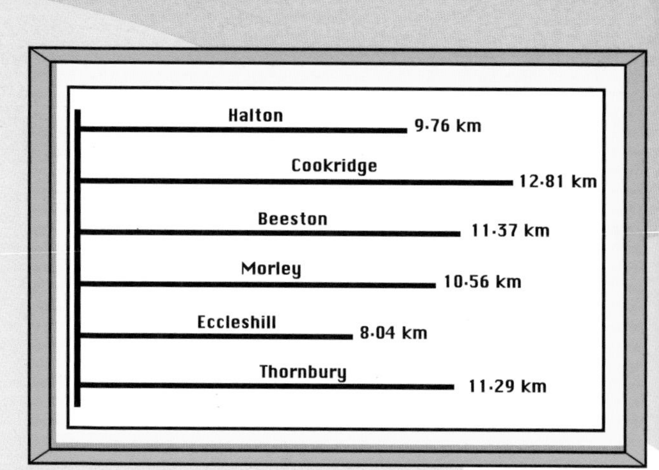

a Sam went on the Halton and Cookridge hikes. What was the total number of kilometres he hiked?

b How much further was the Halton hike than the Eccleshill hike?

c Becky went on 2 hikes. She walked a total distance of 22·66 km. Which hikes did she go on?

d Harry went on 2 hikes. The difference in length was 730 m. Which hikes did he go on?

3 Sarah used the digit cards 4 to 9 to make this addition:

4 · 8 6 + 7 · 5 9

a Work out the answer to Sarah's addition.

b Using the same digits as Sarah, make a similar addition of decimals which gives the largest possible answer.

c Make 3 more additions which also give the largest possible answer.

d Use the same digits to make an addition which gives the smallest possible answer.

e Make 3 more additions which also give the smallest possible answer.

1a In one year Rob makes the same train journey 6 times to watch eagles. The return journey is 372 miles. What is the total distance Rob travels?

b Each return ticket costs £174. What is the total cost of 6 journeys?

2a Maggie is also a bird watcher.
She makes a 48-mile journey 26 times.
How many miles does she travel in total in one year?

b Each of her journeys costs £43. What is the total cost of 26 journeys?

3a How many more miles does Rob travel than Maggie in the year?

b How much more than Rob does Maggie spend on travelling?

4 Work out the first multiplication in each set.
Use it to find the answers to the other multiplications.

a	b	c
77 × 7	11 × 22	123 × 45
770 × 7	110 × 22	12·3 × 45
7·7 × 7	11 × 220	123 × 4·5
0·77 × 7	1·1 × 22	12·3 × 4·5
77 × 0·7	1·1 × 2·2	1·23 × 45
77 × 70	0·11 × 22	12·3 × 0·45
177 × 7	111 × 22	1·23 × 4·5

5 Find what the missing digits in these multiplications could be:

a

```
   7 · □ 7
 ×       6
 ---------
 4 □ · □ 2
```

b

```
   1 □ 9 □
 ×       □
 ---------
 1 2 7 3 6
```

c

```
   □ 8 □
 ×     7
 -------
 4 0 8 □
```

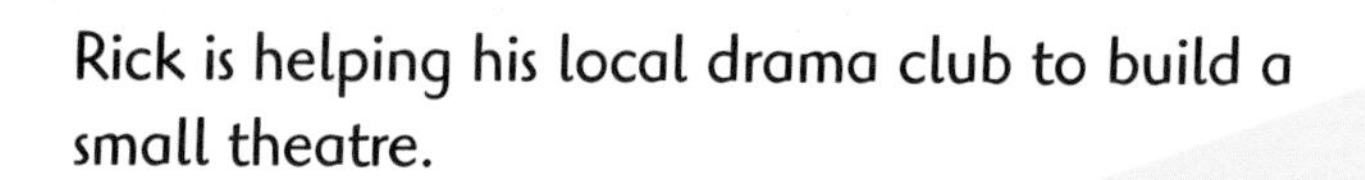

Rick is helping his local drama club to build a small theatre.

1a They bought 6 lengths of 1·45 m skirting board. What was the total length of the 6 pieces?

b Flooring costs £23·20 for every square metre. How much will it cost to floor 8 square metres of the stage?

2 The kitchen area needs tiling. Work out how many 7 cm square tiles are needed to make one row along a wall measuring:

a 185 cm **b** 170 cm.

3 Find the missing numbers in these divisions:

a 70·2 ÷ ☐ = 23·4 **b** 157·6 ÷ ☐ = 19·7

c 214·8 ÷ ☐ = 35·8 **d** 491·4 ÷ ☐ = 54·6

Try rewriting each division as a multiplication.

4 Samantha uses this number machine to make a sequence.

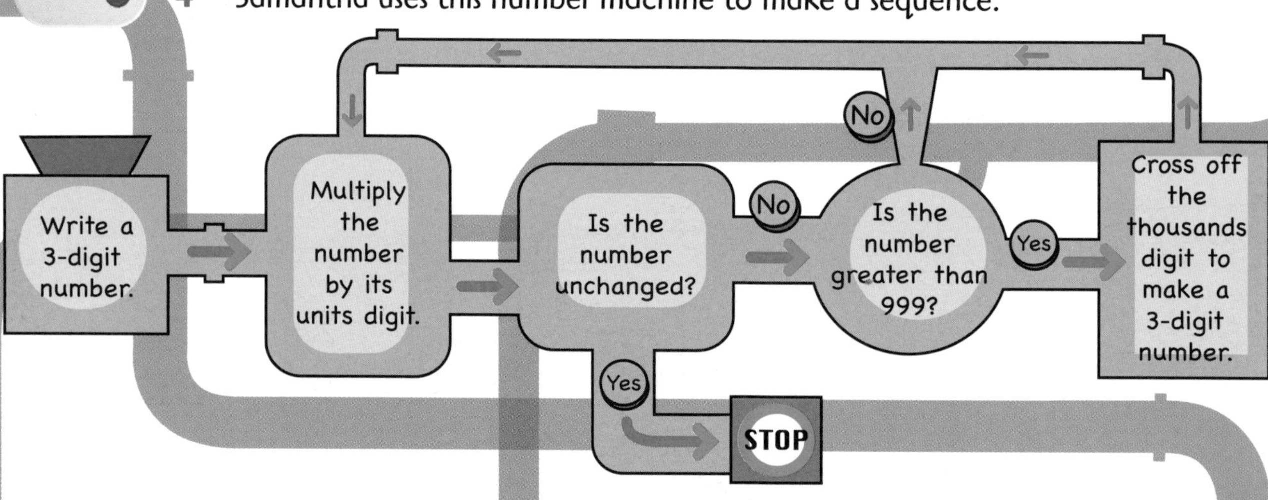

a She starts with the number 253. What is her sequence?

b Find the sequences with these start numbers:

317 841 530 375

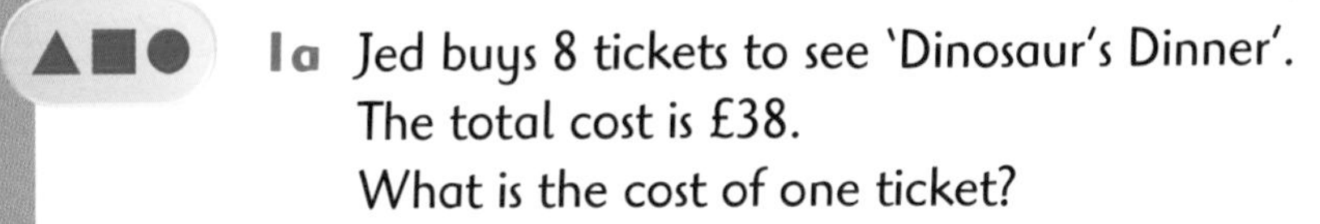

▲■● **1a** Jed buys 8 tickets to see 'Dinosaur's Dinner'. The total cost is £38. What is the cost of one ticket?

b Jane buys 6 tickets to see 'Mystery Manor'. She pays £31·50. How much does one ticket cost?

c The total cost of 9 tickets to see 'Planet Pirates' is £84·15. What is the cost of one ticket?

■● **2** The total cost of 7 tickets in the stalls to see 'Giant Kitten' is £58·10. The total cost for a box for the same number of people is £79·80. How much more does it cost for one person to sit in a box than in the stalls?

3 Choose a number from each spotlight to make divisions with these answers:

a 7·5 **b** 9·5 **c** 3·7 **d** 5·75

Estimate and then check using a calculator.

You need
a calculator

8·51 20·7 17·25 34·2

2·3 3·6

● **4a** Use a calculator to find the answers to 12·3 ÷ 2, 12·3 ÷ 3, ... up to 12·3 ÷ 9.

b Use a calculator and the inverse operation to check the results.

c Explain what happens with each check.

Give as many decimal places as your calculator shows.

1 Draw these mystery triangles.
Sketch them first, then make an accurate drawing.

You need
a ruler
protractor

a a right-angled triangle:
- sides 30 mm, 40 mm and 50 mm long

b an isosceles triangle:
- one side 45 mm long
- two angles of 65°

c an equilateral triangle:
- perimeter 180 mm

d an isosceles triangle:
- one side 55 mm long
- two angles of 50°

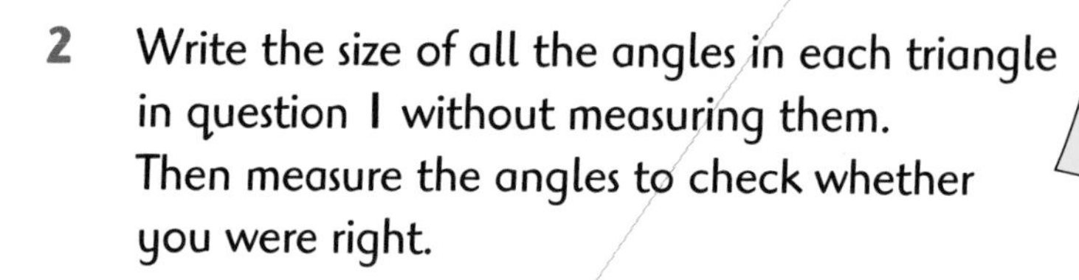

2 Write the size of all the angles in each triangle in question 1 without measuring them.
Then measure the angles to check whether you were right.

Remember that the angles of a triangle add to 180°.

3 Construct these shapes accurately.
Measure and label the length of x in millimetres and the size of angle y in degrees.

You need
a ruler
a protractor

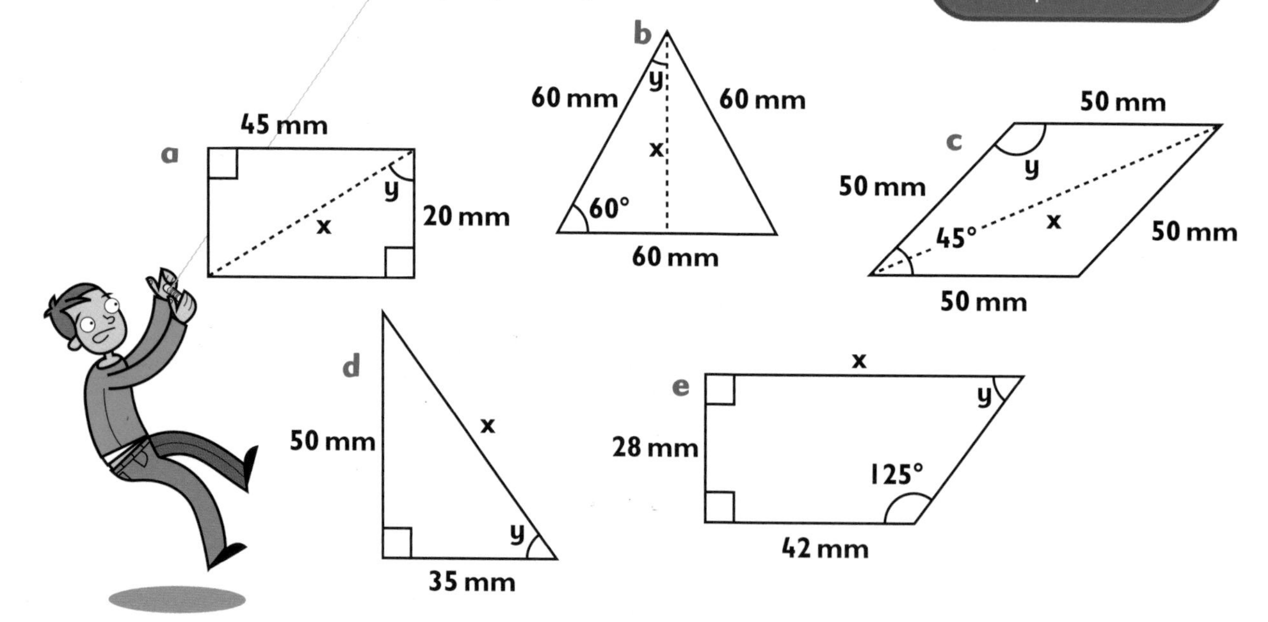

Unit 3 Use a protractor to measure and draw angles to the nearest degree.
Calculate angles in a triangle or around a point.

Rangoli designs are often used in India to decorate floors and walls. They are placed at the entrance to a home to welcome visitors. The symmetrical patterns are often drawn on a grid of dots. Here is one way of designing your own Rangoli patterns.

You need
CM 27
coloured pencils
scissors

1a Draw some straight lines on the 'master grid' on CM 27.

b Copy the lines into the top left-hand section of the design grid. Draw a reflection of this in the top right-hand section.

c Cut out the master grid and turn it 90° clockwise. Copy these lines into the top right-hand section of the design grid.

d Reflect the pattern from the top right-hand section, horizontally and vertically. You now have a symmetrical Rangoli design. Colour it to complete the design.

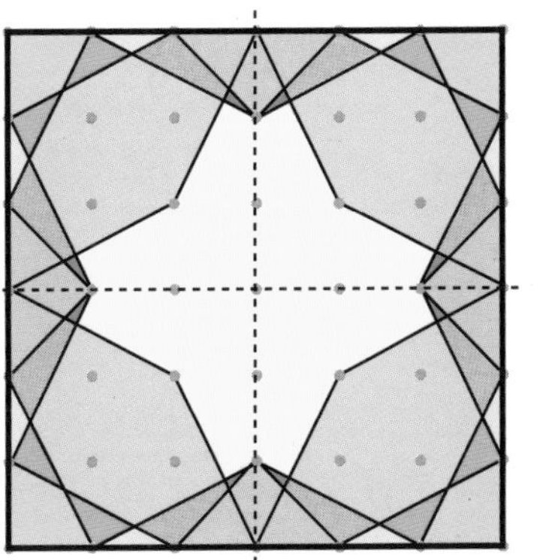

2 Display your design and write about the reflective and rotational symmetry.

1a Make a shape tile on the small square at the bottom of CM 28.

- Cut out the square.
- Cut out a shape.
- Stick the cut-out piece to the opposite side of the square.

b Draw round your shape tile 10 times on coloured paper. Cut out the coloured shapes.

You need
CM 28
coloured paper
scissors
glue and sticky tape

2 Use your coloured shapes to make a wallpaper design.

- Place a shape on the grid on CM 28.
- Place a second shape on the grid so that it is a translation of the first.
- Continue the translation pattern as far as you can.
- Stick your shapes onto the grid.

3 Now make a reflection pattern.
Use another copy of CM 28.
Cut out more coloured shapes if you need to.

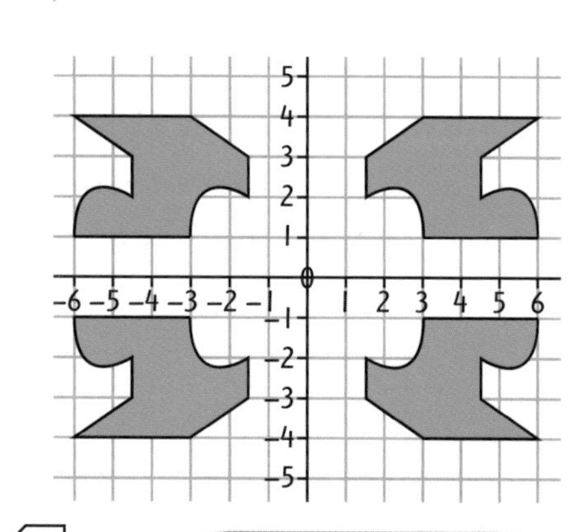

4 Design a new shape tile.

- Cut pieces from 2 sides of a square.
- Stick each cut-out piece to the opposite side.
- Draw round your shape tile on coloured paper.
- Use the shapes to make a tessellating pattern.

You need
plain or
squared paper

1 Cut out the shape generator from CM 29. Carefully fold along the lines so that they all fold both ways.

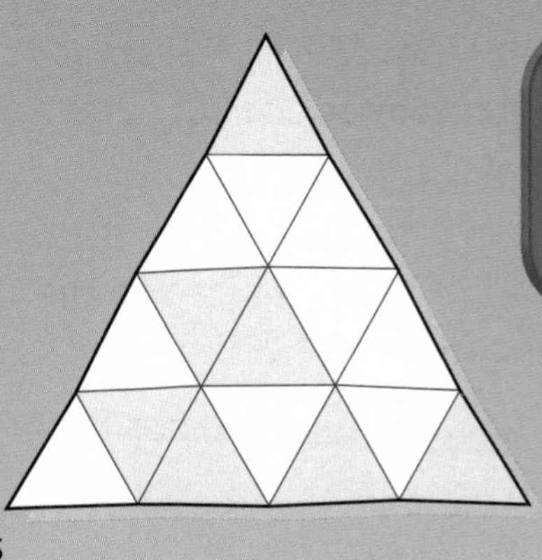

You need
CM 29
CM 30
scissors
a protractor

A quadrilateral is a 2D shape with 4 sides.

a Fold the shape generator to make different quadrilaterals.
Record your quadrilaterals on CM 30.

b Mark the lines of symmetry for each shape.

c For each shape, measure and record the angles.
What is the total of the 4 angles for each shape?

2a Fold the shape generator to make different hexagons.
Record your hexagons on CM 30.

b How many lines of symmetry do they each have?

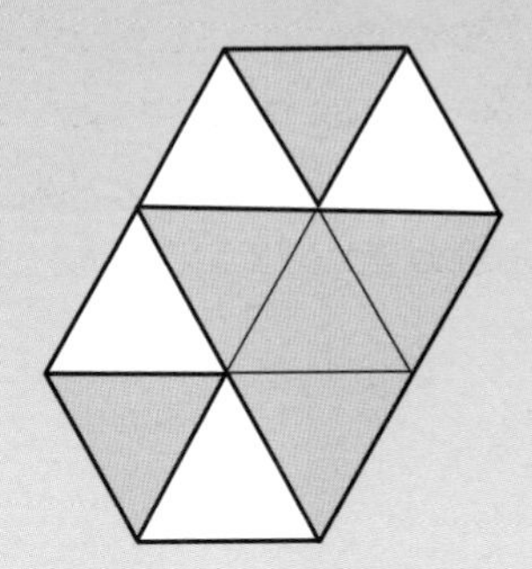

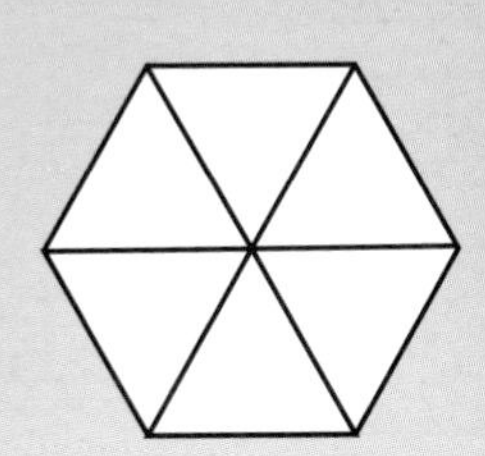

3 Find other shapes. Try making:

a shapes with line symmetry

b shapes with rotational symmetry

c shapes with the same area as others

d shapes with the same perimeter as others

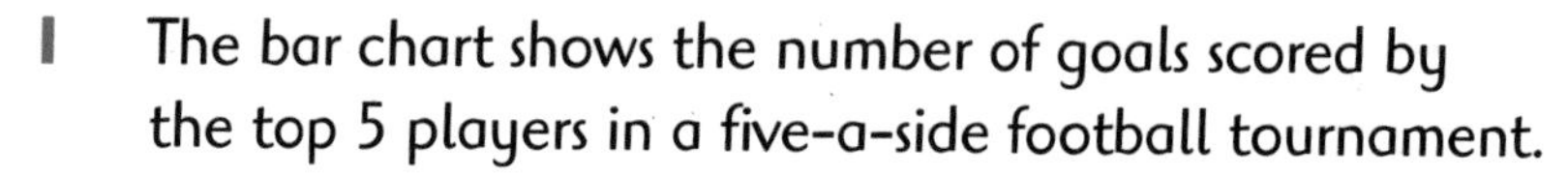

1 The bar chart shows the number of goals scored by the top 5 players in a five-a-side football tournament.

a Find the number of goals scored by each player.

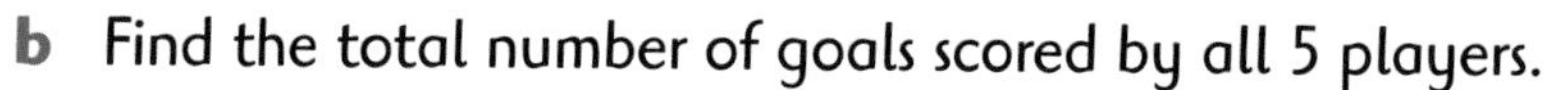

b Find the total number of goals scored by all 5 players.

c How many more goals did Pete score than Florrie?

d How many more goals did Barry need to have equalled Della's score?

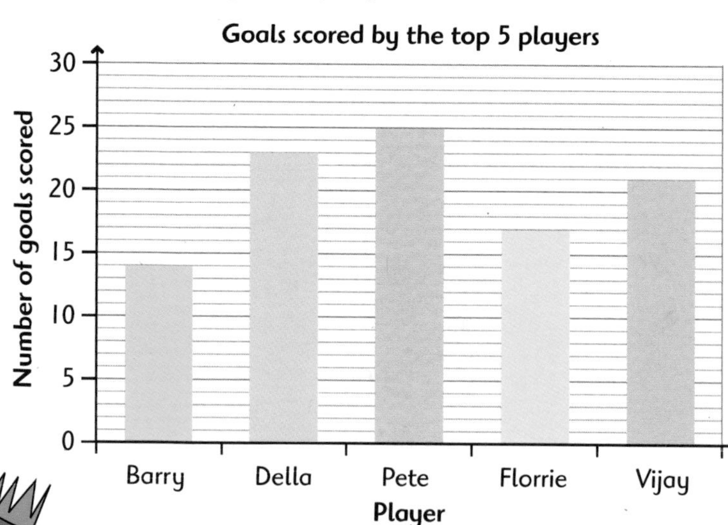

2 This bar chart shows the number of goals scored by all the players in the tournament. For each statement, write whether it is **true** or **false**, or whether it is **impossible to say**.

a 1 player scored more than 24 goals.

b 3 players scored 16 goals.

c 3 players scored 2 goals.

d 2 players scored 11 goals.

e 5 players scored 10 goals or more.

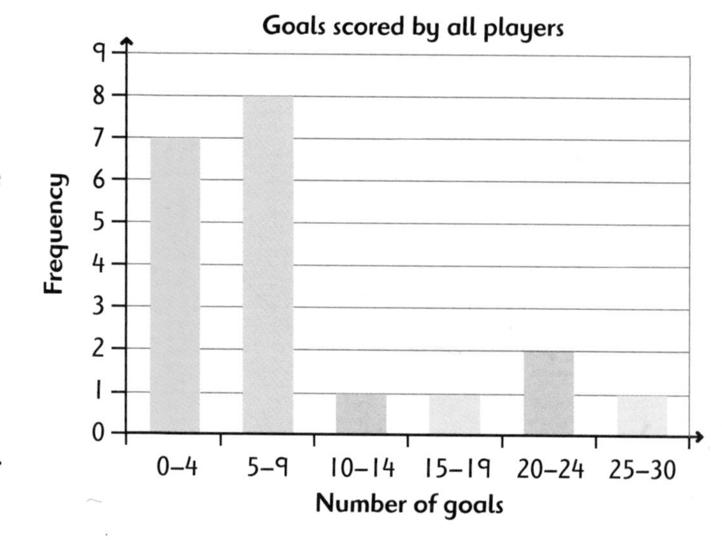

3 Look at CM 31. The big table shows the number of points gained by some teams in the tournament. Some of the information is missing.

a Complete the table.

b Draw a bar chart to show the results.

You need
CM 31
squared paper

1 Last Saturday Ronnie visited the sports club. He cycled there and back.
This graph shows his distance from home.

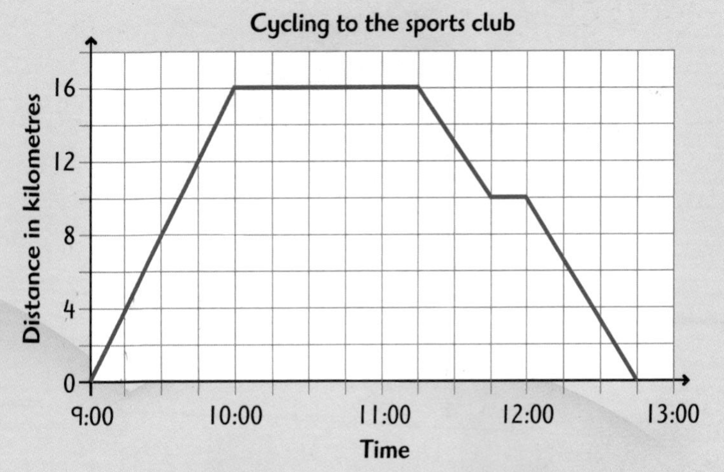

a How far is it from home to the sports club?

b How long did Ronnie spend at the sports club?

c How far had he cycled:
- by 9:15?
- by 9:45?

d How far from home was he at 11:30?

e If Ronnie had not stopped on the way back from the club, when do you think he would have got home?

2 The pie chart shows the canoe lessons given at a watersports centre during the season.

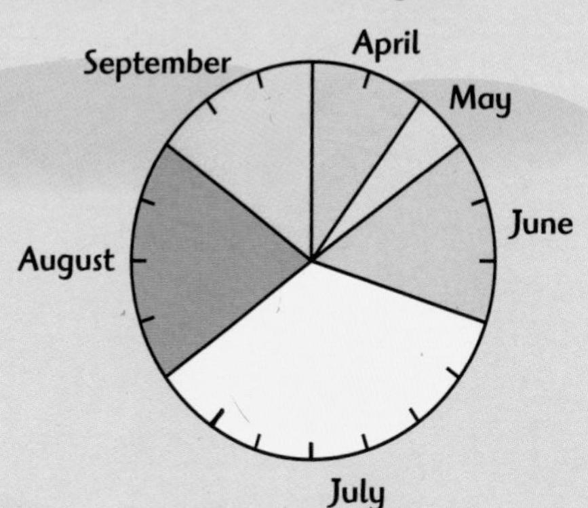

a What percentage of canoe lessons were given:
- in April?
- in July?

b If 150 lessons were given in September, how many were given:
- in May?
- in August?

c How many more lessons were given in July than in June?

3 If the number of lessons given in August was 240, find:

a the number of lessons for each month of the season

b the total amount earned by the watersports centre if it charges £4·50 per lesson.

You need
CM 32

▲■● **1** This table shows the cost of hiring equipment at a ski resort in Colorado.

Item	Cost in US dollars	Cost in UK pounds
boots	\$8	
skis		£10
poles	\$4·80	
snowboard		£6

a Copy and complete the table.
Use the conversion graph on CM 32 to find the missing prices.

b Find the cost in US dollars of hiring:
- skis and poles for 2 days
- a snowboard for 3 days.

■● **2a** Find the cost in US dollars and in UK pounds for:
- a 6-day ski pass costing \$10 per day
- a 5-day hire of one set of boots, skis and poles
- a 3-day hire of snowboards for 4 people.

b The O'Brien family went to Canada for their skiing holiday.
- Draw a conversion graph on CM 31 to show this exchange rate: £1 = Canadian \$2·20.
- Use your graph and your completed table from question 1 to help you find the cost of hiring each item in Canadian dollars.

Put Canadian dollars on the horizontal axis.

● **3a** Round each of these prices to the nearest pound.

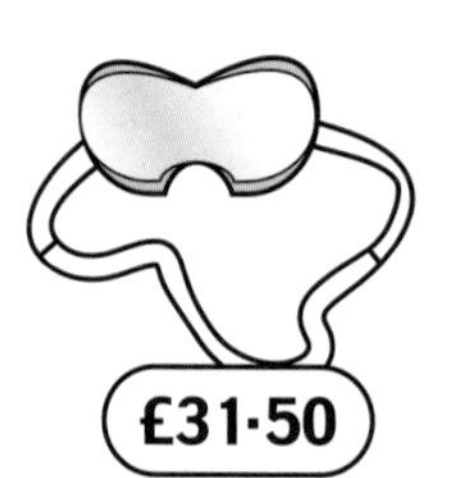

b Find what each item might cost in US dollars.

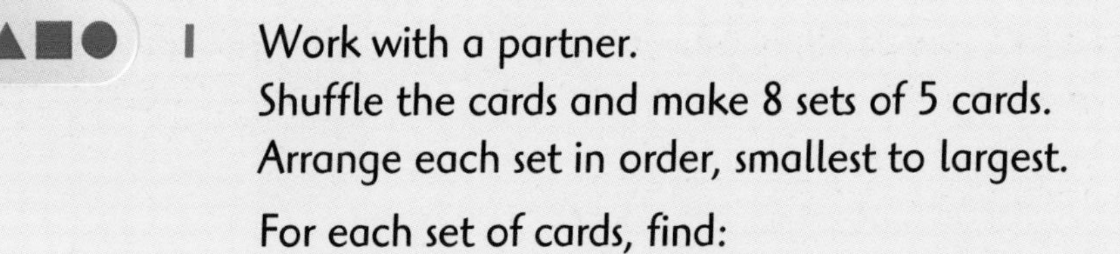

1 Work with a partner.
Shuffle the cards and make 8 sets of 5 cards.
Arrange each set in order, smallest to largest.

You need
4 sets of 1–10 number cards

For each set of cards, find:

a the median
b the range
c the mode
d the mean.

There might be more than one mode, or no mode.
For 2, 2, 3, 4, 4 the modes are 2 and 4.
For 2, 3, 4, 5, 6 there is no mode.

The median is 5.
Range: $10 - 2 = 8$
Mode: 5
Mean: $(2 + 5 + 5 + 9 + 10) = 31$
$31 \div 5 = 6{\cdot}2$

2 Repeat question 1, this time making 5 sets of 7 cards.

3 Megan chose 7 cards from a pile of 2 sets of 1–10 number cards.
She arranged them in order.

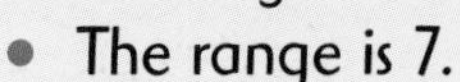

- The range is 7.
- The median is 6.
- The mean is 6.
- There is one mode, 5.

What are the values of her cards?

4 The weather centre at a Cornish beach recorded information about the temperature at noon on 7 days.

Range: 12°C

Mode: 20°C

Median: 18°C

Mean: 19°C

Lowest noon temperature: 15°C

Find the 7 temperatures.

Each temperature is a whole number of degrees.

1 **Units Families** is a game for groups of 3 or 4. It is like 'Happy Families', using the cards from CM 33 and CM 34. Each family has 4 cards, A to D, all about conversions between the same 2 units. The aim is to collect complete families of cards.

You need
cards from CM 33 and CM 34

Put the 4 cards face up in front of you as soon as you get a complete family.

A B C D

120 g ≈ ? oz

30 g ≈ 1 oz

Play the game like this:

- Shuffle the cards and deal them all out.
  All look at your own cards and decide which families you will try to collect.
- Take turns to ask any other player for a card.

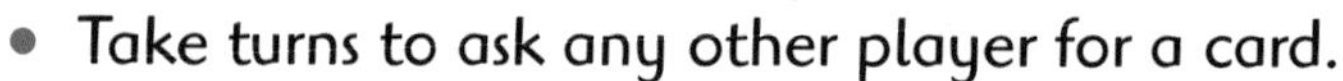

For example, you might ask, 'Shona, do you have card B for grams and ounces?'

- If they have the card, they must show it to you, and you must answer the conversion problem on it.

There is a clue on each card to help you.

- If everyone agrees your answer is correct, you get the card and another turn.
- If they do not have the card, or if your answer was wrong, your turn is over.

The game finishes when all the cards are in families.
The winner is the player with the biggest number of complete families.

2 Make cards for your own **Prices Families** game.
Use prices for different quantities of some foods, rather than units conversions.
Use your cards to play the game.

You could choose from these prices, or make up your own:

apples	*1 kg for 90p*
olives	*100 g for 75p*
cola	*330 ml for 66p*
cheese	*50 g for 60p*
cherries	*200 g for 40p*
crisps	*30 g for 25p*

Winston sleeps for different lengths of time during term-time and in the school holidays.

Term-time

Sunday to Thursday:
Go to bed at 9:15 pm.
Asleep at 9:40 pm.
Wake up the next day at 6:20 am.

Friday and Saturday:
Asleep at 10:30 pm.
Wake up the next day at 8:20 am.

Holidays
Asleep for 10 hours every night.

1a Write each time in the term-time lists as a 24-hour clock time.

b Draw a 24-hour timeline for term-time.
- Start and finish your timeline at noon.
- Write the Sunday to Thursday times above the line, and the Friday and Saturday times below it.

Sunday to Thursday

Noon — Midnight — Noon

Friday and Saturday

2a Use the timeline to find how long Winston:
- sleeps each night in term-time
- spends in bed each night before a school day.

b How long does he spend asleep at night during one week of the holidays?

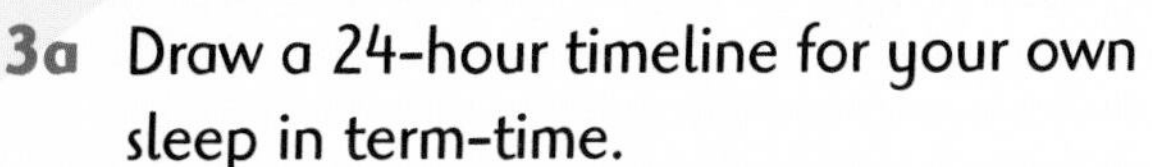

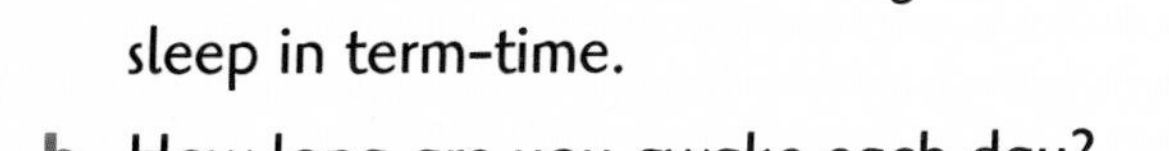

3a Draw a 24-hour timeline for your own sleep in term-time.

b How long are you awake each day?

4a How long does Winston spend asleep in one week:
- in term-time?
- in the holidays?

b What fraction of the week does Winston spend asleep:
- in term-time?
- in the holidays?

Don't forget to cancel to find the simplest fraction.

5 There are 39 weeks in the school year. Write how much time Winston spends asleep over a whole year (52 weeks):

a in hours **b** in days and hours **c** in weeks and days.

You need a calculator

1 ♦ and ♠ stand for positive whole numbers.

a Find all the ways to complete ♦ + ♠ = 10.

b What if ♦ + ♠ = 10, and ♦ is 4 more than ♠?
Look at your answers to **a** to find ♦ and ♠.

c Write your own puzzle for ♦ and ♠ that has only one answer.
Swap puzzles with a partner and solve them.

2a The rule for a sequence is: Start with 1. Add 2 each time.

- Write the first 6 numbers in the sequence.
- Describe the numbers in the sequence.

b Look at the sequence machine.

Put in n = 1, 2, 3 ... 6.

Write the output numbers as a sequence.

Compare the sequence with **a**.
What do you notice?

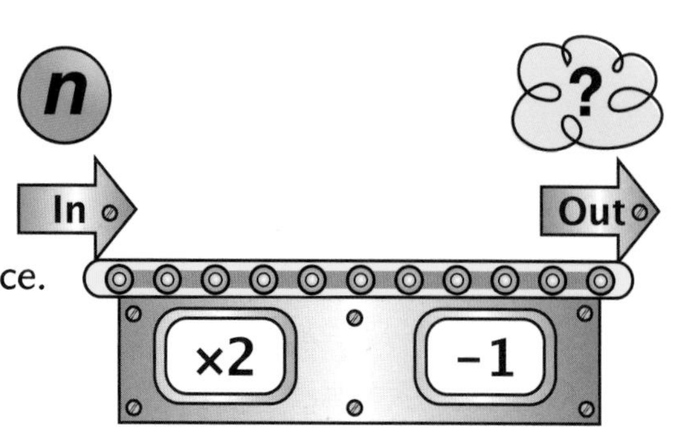

c Design a sequence machine that makes even numbers.

3a Copy and complete the table to find the first 4 terms in a sequence.

n	$3n - 1$
1	2
2	
3	
4	

b Write the sequence, and continue it for 3 more terms.

c What is the rule for the sequence?

4 p and q stand for positive whole numbers.

a Find what numbers p and q might stand for here: $p \times q = 24$

b What if $p \times q = 24$ and $p - q = 5$?
Look at your answers to part **a** to find p and q.

c Write your own puzzle for p and q that has only one answer.
Swap puzzles with a partner and solve them.

1 Here are 4 incomplete calculations:

a	♦ + ♠ = 18	**b**	♥ + ♣ = 10
c	20 – ♣ = ♦	**d**	♦ × ♥ = ♠

Key

- ♥ an even number
- ♣ a multiple of 3
- ♦ a multiple of 4
- ♠ a multiple of 5

- All the missing numbers are positive and are 40 or smaller.
- The value of a symbol might not be the same in different calculations.

Find the missing numbers to complete each calculation. Show your working.

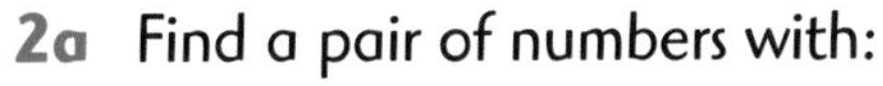

2a Find a pair of numbers with:
- a sum of 15 and a product of 56
- a sum of 115 and a product of 3306.

b Write what you notice about each pair.

You need a calculator

3a Find 3 consecutive numbers with a sum of:
- 6
- 27
- 39.

b Find all the factors of each of the sums in part **a**.

c Write about what you notice. Is there a rule for the sum of any 3 consecutive numbers? Explain your answer.

4a Use square numbers to complete ■ – ■ = ■.

b Use triangular numbers to complete ▲ – ▲ = ▲.

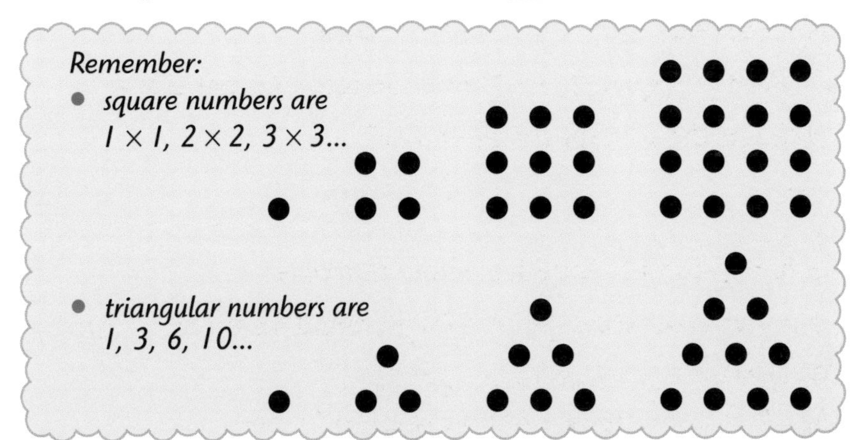

5 Look at CM 35.
Follow the instructions to make magic diamonds.

You need CM 35

1 At the school fair, 4 children play 4 different games 10 times each. Each time a game is played, children score points if they come first or second.
Work out how many points are awarded for first place and how many for second place in each kind of game.

Frisbee hurling

Name	First places	Second places	Total points scored
Miles	2	2	8
Nerys	5	1	16
Olivia	3	1	10
Punit	0	6	6

Duck fishing

Name	First places	Second places	Total points scored
Miles	3	1	11
Nerys	3	0	9
Olivia	2	5	16
Punit	2	4	14

Hoopla

Name	First places	Second places	Total points scored
Miles	1	7	18
Nerys	2	2	12
Olivia	2	1	10
Punit	5	0	20

Shove penny

Name	First places	Second places	Total points scored
Miles	3	1	7
Nerys	1	4	6
Olivia	2	4	8
Punit	4	1	9

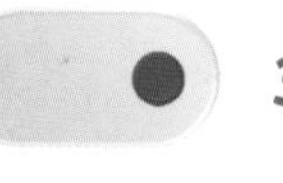

2 The children agree that it would be fairer if 4 points were given for first place and 3 points for second place in each game.

a How many points would each player have scored in each game with this system?

b What would each child's total score for the 40 games have been?

3 Next the children played at the coconut shy 20 times.
Look at the results.
Work out how many points are awarded for first, second and third places.
Show your working.

Coconut shy

Name	First places	Second places	Third places	Total points scored
Miles	3	8	0	39
Nerys	7	3	10	54
Olivia	3	8	1	40
Punit	7	1	9	47

1a Alex makes a mystery number grid. He rings 2 numbers, one from each row, but from different columns. What is the sum of his 2 numbers?

82	(41)
(59)	18

You need
CM 36
coloured pencils

b Add together the other 2 numbers.
Is the sum the same?
What do you think is the mystery number for this grid?

2 What are the mystery numbers of these grids?
Use CM 36 to help you work.

Find pairs of numbers with the same total.

64	21
79	36

5·8	1·3
8·7	4·2

2·1	2·5
7·5	7·9

0·18	0·56
0·44	0·82

3 Alex makes some larger mystery grids.

a Ring 3 numbers from each grid on CM 36, from different rows and columns.

4·8	6·1	3·4
2·3	3·6	0·9
3	4·3	1·6

17·9	44·2	24·8
39·4	65·7	46·3
9·5	35·8	16·4

3·26	4·62	2·75
4·42	5·78	3·91
1·47	2·83	0·96

b Predict the mystery number of each grid.

c Test your prediction.

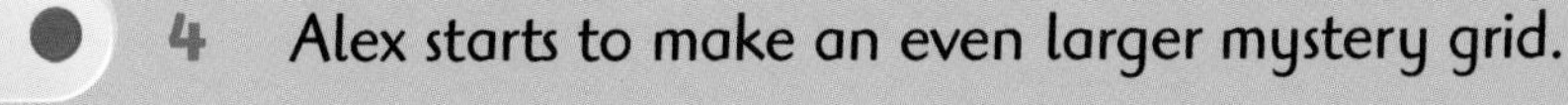

4 Alex starts to make an even larger mystery grid.

a Work with a friend to complete the mystery grid on CM 36.

b Predict its mystery number.

c Test your prediction.

1 There are 9 races at the Woodford Cycling Championships.
The table shows each rider's times in the first 6 races.

Rider	Race 1	Race 2	Race 3	Race 4	Race 5	Race 6
Harris	23 min 17·4 s	27 min 59·3 s	32 min 12·3 s	18 min 58·8 s	37 min 23·4 s	24 min 7·4 s
Waltob	23 min 19·5 s	27 min 58·1 s	32 min 27·5 s	18 min 59·5 s	37 min 22·9 s	24 min 7·1 s
Kirkdale	23 min 14·7 s	28 min 12·5 s	32 min 19·7 s	19 min 0·1 s	37 min 35·7 s	24 min 0·6 s
Fresher	23 min 14·2 s	28 min 1·2 s	32 min 33·6 s	19 min 1·6 s	37 min 23·1 s	24 min 10·1 s
Granger	23 min 12·4 s	27 min 58·8 s	32 min 27·1 s	18 min 59·4 s	37 min 30 s	24 min 11·1 s
Manston	23 min 15·9 s	28 min 18·2 s	32 min 22·9 s	19 min 0·9 s	37 min 24·2 s	24 min 6·9 s

a Find the winner of each race.

b This table shows the number of points given for each position in a race.

Finish position	1st	2nd	3rd	4th	5th	6th
Points	21	15	10	6	3	1

Make a table to show the number of points each rider gained for each race.

c How many points did each rider gain altogether for these 6 races?

2 This table shows the total points for each rider after all 9 races.

a Use your answer to question 1c to find how many points each rider gained for the last 3 races.

b How many times did each rider finish first, second ... in these 3 races?

c What might the finishing order for each of the last 3 races have been?

Rider	Total points after 9 races
Harris	102
Waltob	94
Kirkdale	93
Fresher	55
Granger	80
Manston	80

Albrecht Dürer was a famous artist who worked in Germany in the 15th and 16th centuries.
He also created this very special magic square.

16	3	2	13
5	10	11	8
9	6	7	12
4	15	14	1

1a Find the sum of each row of 4 numbers.

b Find the sum of each column.

c Find the sum of each of the 2 diagonals.

d Look at the square on the right.
Find the sum of the set of 4 numbers coloured:

- red
- blue
- green
- yellow.

16	3	2	13
5	10	11	8
9	6	7	12
4	15	14	1

2 What is special about the numbers coloured red and blue in this square?

16	3	2	13
5	10	11	8
9	6	7	12
4	15	14	1

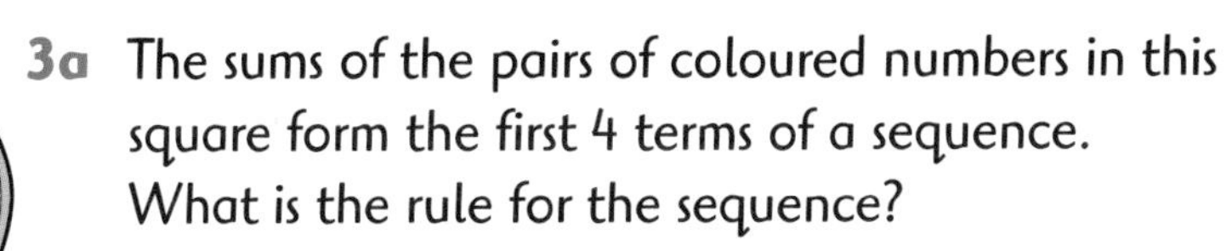

3a The sums of the pairs of coloured numbers in this square form the first 4 terms of a sequence.
What is the rule for the sequence?

b Write about any other patterns you can see in Dürer's magic square.

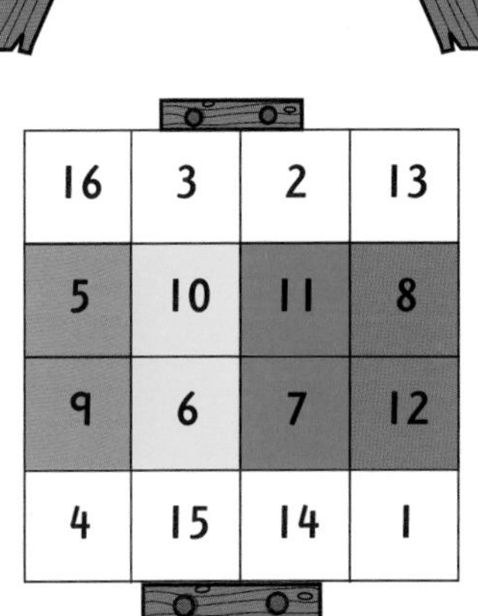

16	3	2	13
5	10	11	8
9	6	7	12
4	15	14	1

4a Find as many ways as you can of making 34 by adding 4 numbers from 1 to 16.
Do not use any number more than once in an addition.

b Colour some of your sets of 4 numbers on the Dürer magic squares on CM 37. Join the 4 coloured numbers to make a quadrilateral, then name the quadrilateral.

You need
CM 37
coloured pencils

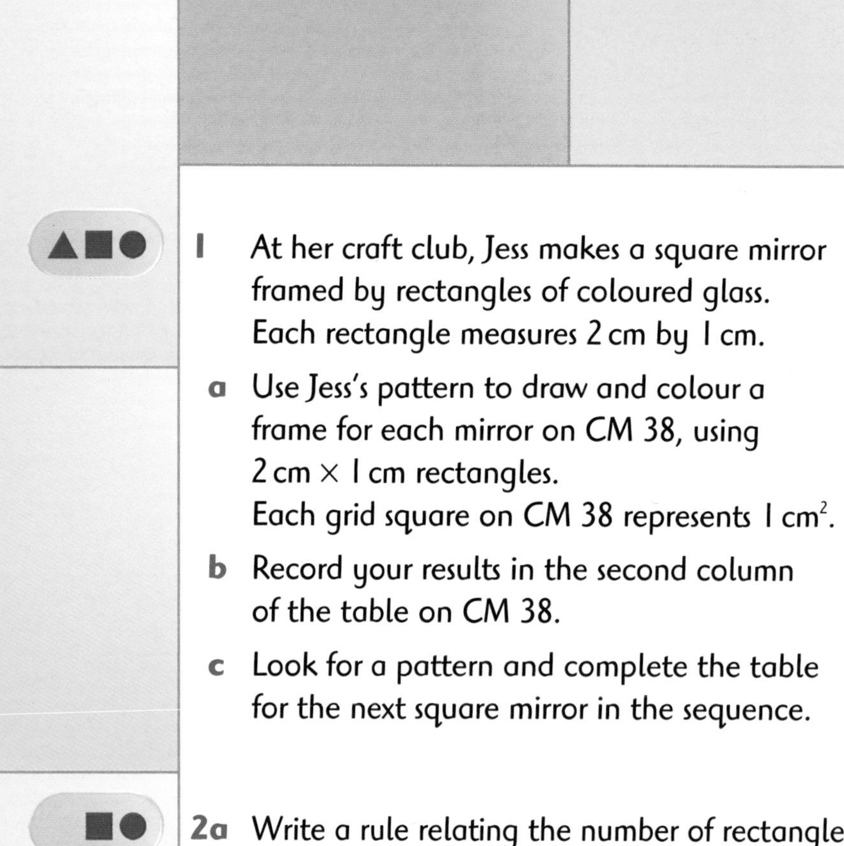

1 At her craft club, Jess makes a square mirror framed by rectangles of coloured glass. Each rectangle measures 2 cm by 1 cm.

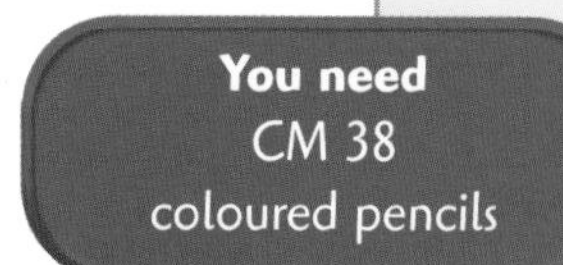

a Use Jess's pattern to draw and colour a frame for each mirror on CM 38, using 2 cm × 1 cm rectangles.
Each grid square on CM 38 represents 1 cm^2.

b Record your results in the second column of the table on CM 38.

c Look for a pattern and complete the table for the next square mirror in the sequence.

2a Write a rule relating the number of rectangles (N) needed to frame each square mirror on CM 38 to its side length (L). Test your rule.

b Find the area of the frame for each mirror on CM 38. Record your results in the table.

c Tim uses 42 rectangles, measuring 2 cm by 1 cm, to make a frame for a square mirror. What size is the mirror?

d Each coloured rectangle costs 19p. What is the cost of Tim's frame?

3 Terry buys 12 identical rectangular tiles. She fits them round a square mirror like this. For one of the rectangular tiles, find:

a its length and breadth

b its area and perimeter.

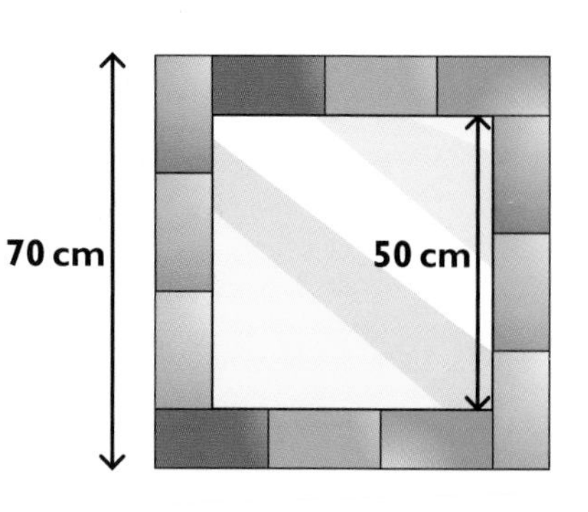

You need
1 cm cubes

1a Use 1 cm cubes to make each of these cubes:

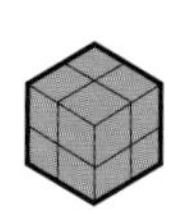
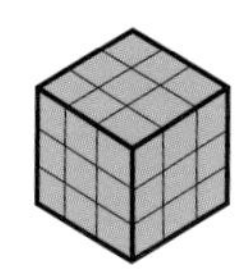

b Find the surface area of each cube.

First find the area of one face.

2 This is the net of a cube.
Find its surface area.

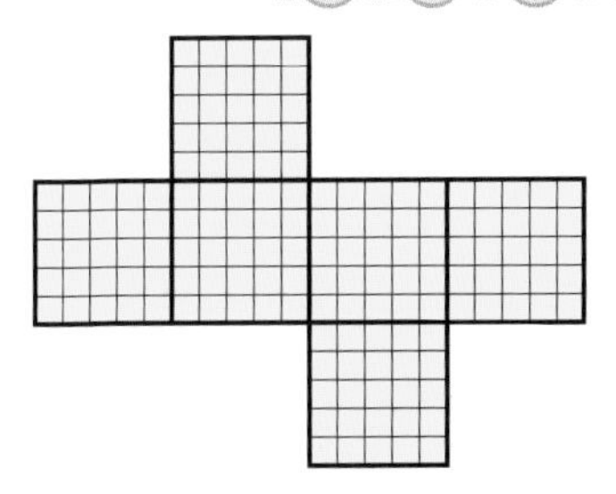

You need
1 cm cubes
1 cm squared paper

3 This is the net of a cuboid. Work with a partner.

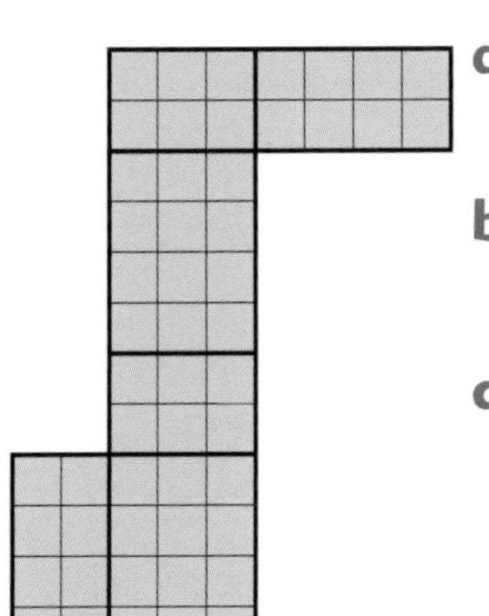

a Use the net to find the surface area of the cuboid.

b Build the cuboid to check your answer.

c Using the same number of cubes:
- build 2 different cuboids
- draw their nets on 1 cm squared paper
- use the nets to find the surface area of each cuboid.

You need
1 cm squared paper

4 The box for a cycle helmet is a cube with sides 30 cm long.

a Design a cube container to hold 64 cycle helmet boxes. Draw the net of your container on squared paper.

Find its surface area.

b Now design a cuboid container to hold 64 helmet boxes. Draw the net of your container.

Find its surface area.

c Which container has the smaller surface area?

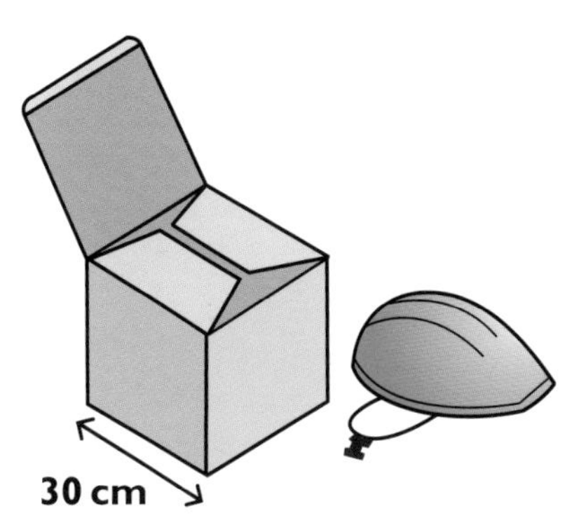

1 The plan shows a square softball diamond at the centre of a square grass pitch.

a Find the area of the softball diamond.

b Find the area of the grass surrounding the softball diamond.

c Repeat parts **a** and **b** for:

- a diamond with 15 m sides and a pitch with 35 m sides.
- a diamond with 21 m sides and a pitch with 38 m sides.

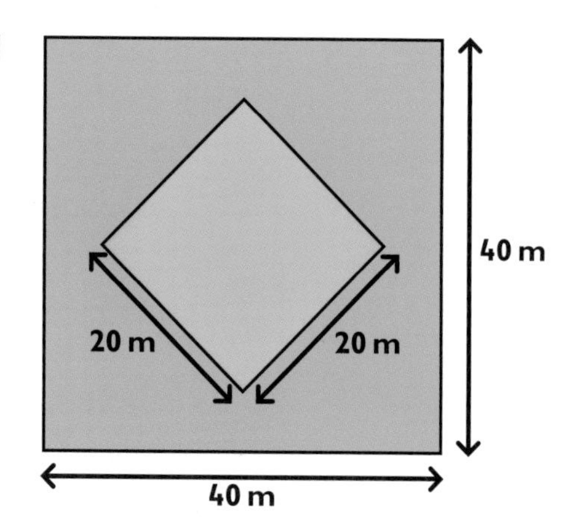

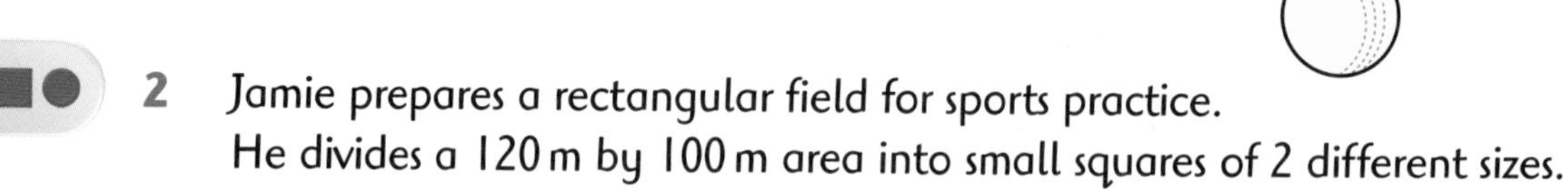

2 Jamie prepares a rectangular field for sports practice.
He divides a 120 m by 100 m area into small squares of 2 different sizes.

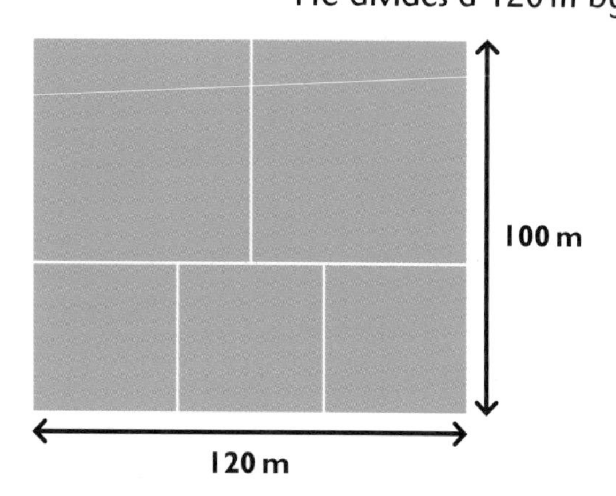

a Find the perimeter and area of:

- one of the smaller squares
- one of the larger squares.

b One of the larger squares is reserved for high-jump practice. For the remaining area, calculate:

- its area
- its perimeter.

3 An international athletics competition is held at a sports ground.
Work out the area of white in each country's flag.

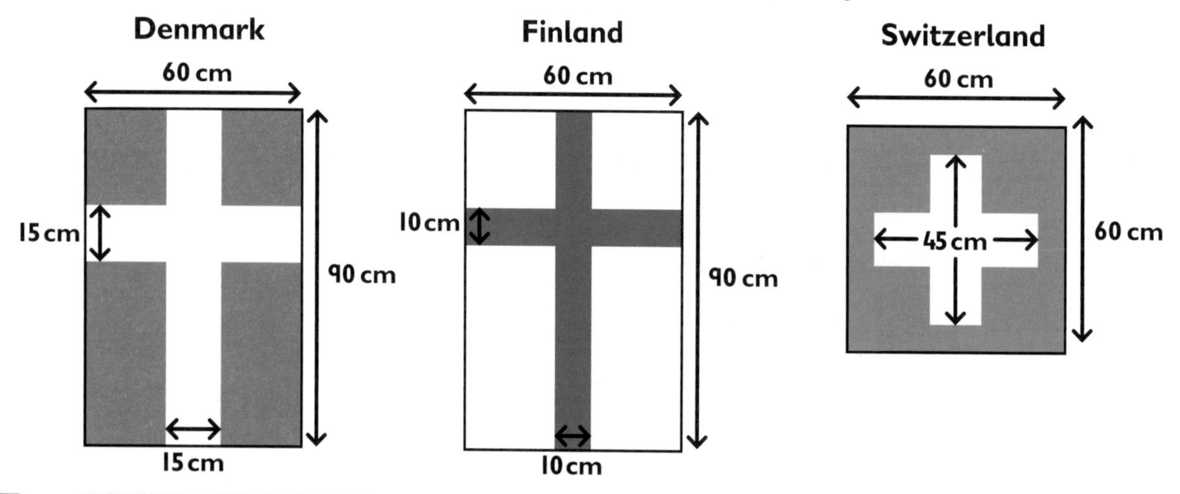

1 Play **Count On** in groups of 3 or 4.

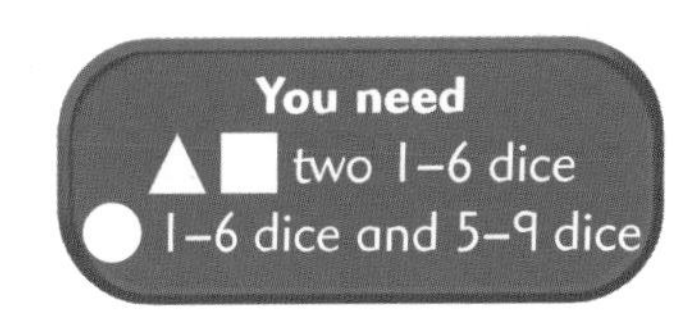

- Take turns to be the counter in each round.
- The counter rolls both dice and adds the numbers to make the **count number**.
- Each player then takes a turn to roll both dice, choose one of the numbers shown, and record it as their **digit**.
- The counter then counts out loud from 0 in steps of the count number, stopping after the 12th step.
- Each player makes a tally mark every time their digit appears in the numbers called out. This gives their **score**.

For example, if a 2 and a 3 are thrown, the count number is 5.

For example, if the count number is 5, they say '5, 10, 15, 20, 25 ... 60'.

Play another 11 rounds like this.

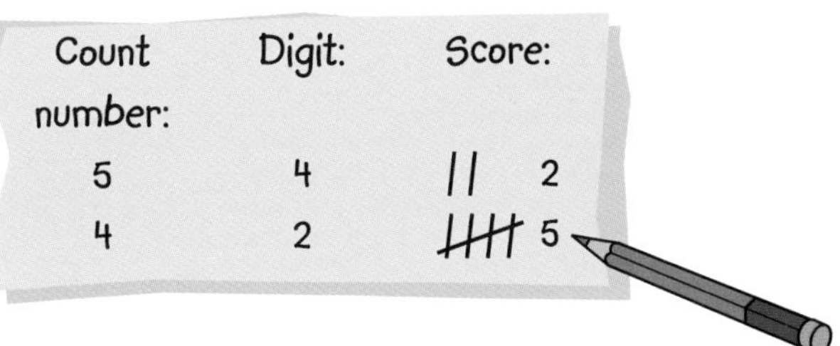

Count number:	Digit:	Score:
5	4	// 2
4	2	~~////~~ 5

2 For one round, Max wrote the score for his digit as a **proportion** of the number of steps in the count (12).

a Do the same for each of your scores.

b Compare your proportions with other players.

Count number:	Digit:	Score:	Proportion:
5	4	// 2	$\frac{2}{12} = \frac{1}{6}$
4	2	~~////~~ 5	$\frac{5}{12}$

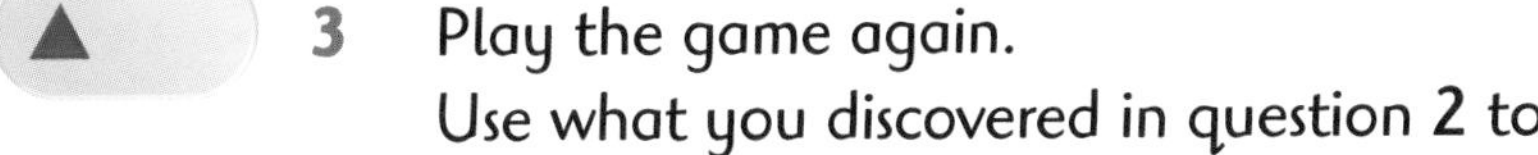

3 Play the game again.
Use what you discovered in question **2** to try and score more.

4a Which digit would you expect to appear in the greatest proportion?

b What if you only counted for 10 steps, not 12?
Does this digit change?

c Play the game again, counting for a different number of steps.
Try to score more.

Play **Trade Up** in groups of 3 or 4.
See how much money you can make from selling 3 different items.

You need
gameboard on CM 39
cards from CM 40 and CM 41
record table from CM 41
a dice
a counter, a calculator

First, get ready:

- Place the item cards face up in their boxes on the gameboard (CM 39).
- Place the profit cards (P) face up in a pile.
- Place the discount cards (D) face up in a pile.

1. Take turns to roll the dice and move your counter. You will land on a 1, a 2 or a 3. This tells you which item you are selling.
2. Look in the item box to see how much it will cost you. Record the **cost price** in the table on CM 41.
3. Pick up a profit card (P) from the top of the pile. Increase the cost of your item by the percentage on the card to give the full price. Record the **profit** (percentage) and **full price** in your table. Replace the profit card at the bottom of the pile.
4. If you landed on a ☆, you are having a sale! Pick up a discount card (D) from the top of the pile. Reduce the full price by the percentage on the card to give your final price. Record the **discount** (percentage) and **final price** in your table. Replace the discount card at the bottom of the pile.
5. If you did not land on a ☆, record your full price as the **final price** in your table.
6. Subtract the cost price from your final price to find your **overall profit or loss** on this item. Record it in your table.

Put + if you made a profit or – if you made a loss.

Shuffle the profit and discount cards at the end of each round.

The game finishes when one player lands exactly on Finish.
Add up all your overall profits and losses.
The winner is the player who has made the most money altogether.

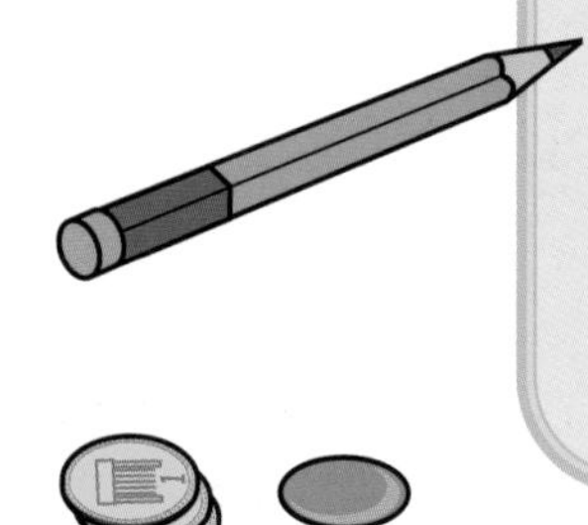

Look at the example opposite to help you.

I threw a 5 and landed on a square marked 2.

Item 2 was the guitar.
It cost £100.
I wrote '£100' under 'Cost price' in my table.

Next I picked up a profit card.
I had to add 50% to the cost price.

50% of £100 = £50
£100 + £50 = £150
The full price is £150

The square I landed on had a ☆, so I had to pick up a discount card.
I had to take 25% off the full price.

25% of £150 = £37·50
£150 − £37·50 = £112·50
The final price is £112·50

Next, I found the overall profit or loss.

£112·50 − £100 = £12·50

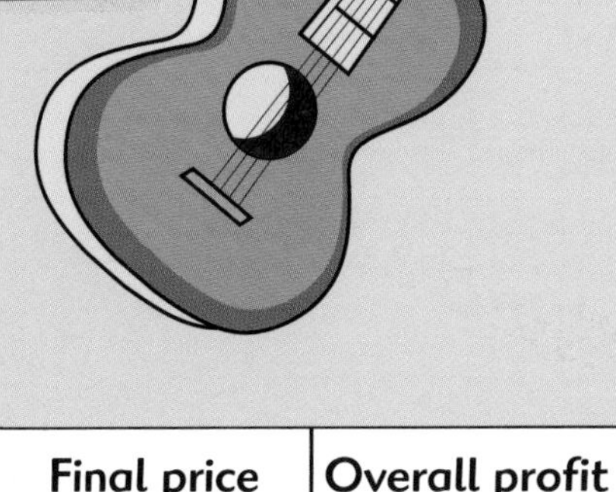

I made an overall profit of £12·50. Here's how I recorded my turn.

Cost price	Profit (percentage)	Full price	Discount (percentage)	Final price	Overall profit or loss
£100	50%	£150	25%	£112·50	£12·50

1 Paper sizes use the names A0, A1, A2, A3 ...
Each paper size is half as big as the size before it.

Write as a fraction the proportion of an A0 sheet covered by:

- an A1 sheet
- an A2 sheet
- an A3 sheet
- an A4 sheet
- an A5 sheet
- an A6 sheet.

You need
CM 42
A4 paper
sticky tape
a long ruler
a calculator

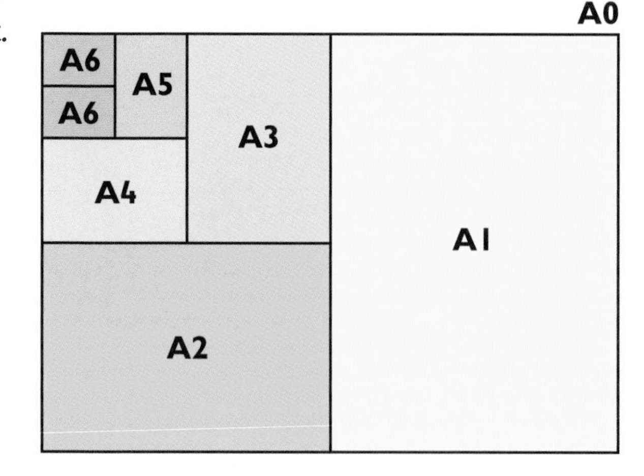

2a Take a piece of A4 paper.
Measure its length and width in millimetres.
Record the measurements on CM 42.

b Carefully fold the A4 paper in half so the 2 short edges meet exactly. This size is called A5.
Measure its length and width in millimetres and record the measurements on CM 42.

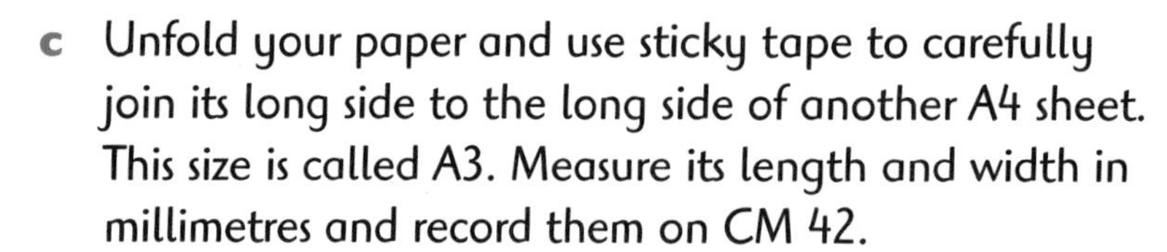

c Unfold your paper and use sticky tape to carefully join its long side to the long side of another A4 sheet.
This size is called A3. Measure its length and width in millimetres and record them on CM 42.

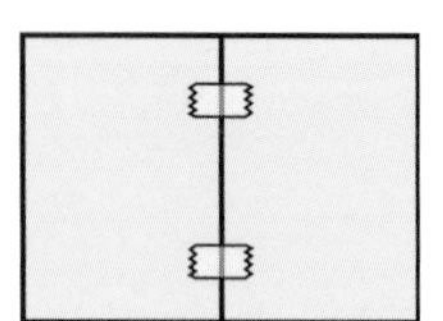

d For each paper size you have measured, use a calculator to divide the length by the width.
Record the answers to 1 decimal place on CM 42.

e What do you notice about the ratio of length to width each time?
Complete the ratio statement on CM 42.

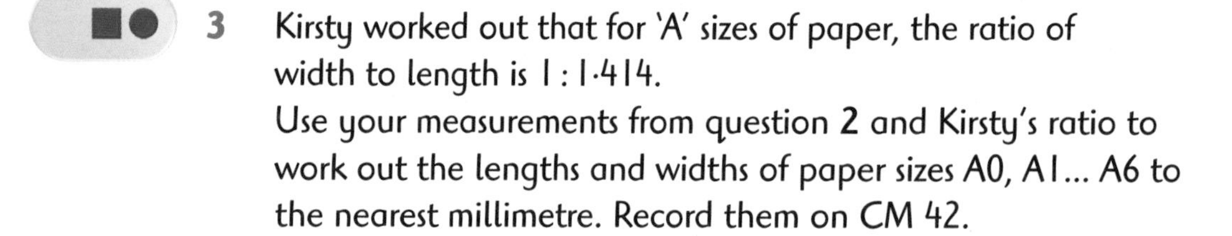

3 Kirsty worked out that for 'A' sizes of paper, the ratio of width to length is 1 : 1·414.
Use your measurements from question **2** and Kirsty's ratio to work out the lengths and widths of paper sizes A0, A1... A6 to the nearest millimetre. Record them on CM 42.

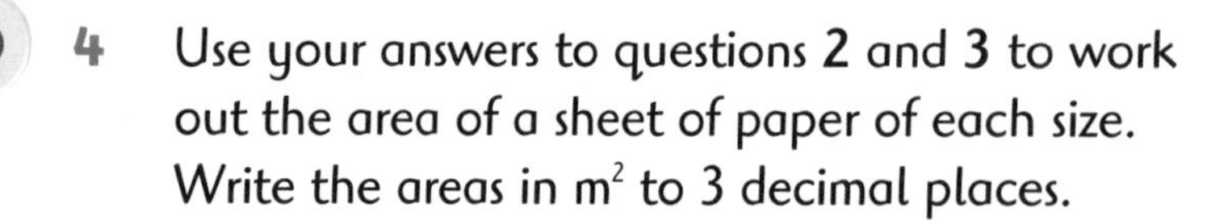

4 Use your answers to questions **2** and **3** to work out the area of a sheet of paper of each size.
Write the areas in m^2 to 3 decimal places.

$1\ m^2 = 1\ 000\ 000\ mm^2$
$0{\cdot}000\ 001\ m^2 = 1\ mm^2$.

A group of friends play pinball.

- If a ball falls into one of the target holes, the player scores that number of points.
- If a ball misses all the targets, it falls to the bottom and the player scores nothing.
- Each player has 5 balls to play.

1a Helen scored 0, 2, 8, 16 and 0.
What was her total score?

b Guy scored 31.
Which targets did he hit?

c Kim scored 10.
Which targets did she hit?

d All Kiara's balls scored in the same target, giving her a total of 80.
Which target did they hit?

e When Kevin played, 2 balls went into one target and 3 into another target.
His total score was 50.
Which 2 targets did he hit?

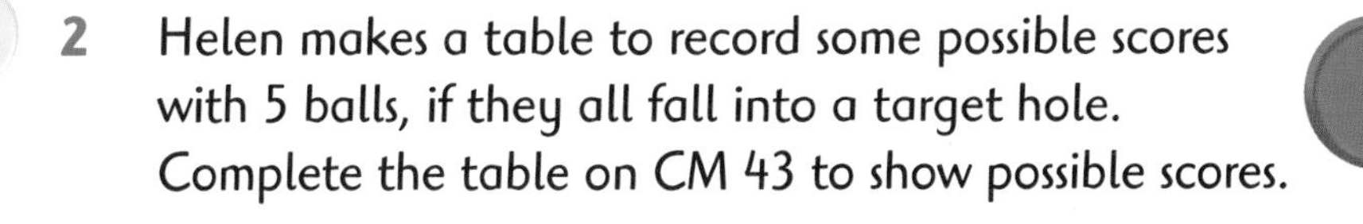

2 Helen makes a table to record some possible scores with 5 balls, if they all fall into a target hole.
Complete the table on CM 43 to show possible scores.

You need
CM 43

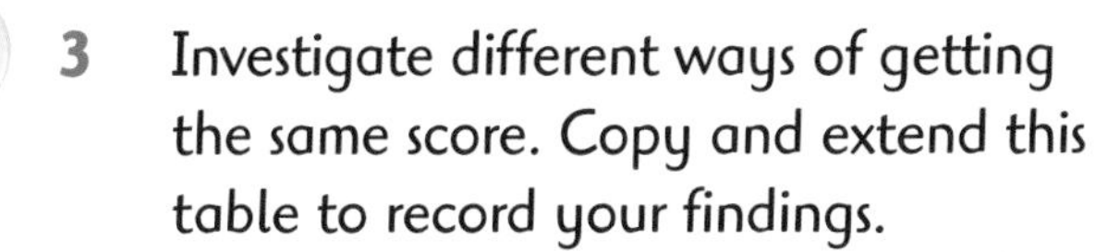

3 Investigate different ways of getting the same score. Copy and extend this table to record your findings.

Total score	Ways of scoring
1	1 + 0 + 0 + 0 + 0
2	1 + 1 + 0 + 0 + 0
2	2 + 0 + 0 + 0 + 0

A	1
B	2
C	3
D	4
E	5
F	6
G	7
H	8
I	9
J	10
K	11
L	12
M	13
N	14
O	15
P	16
Q	17
R	18
S	19
T	20
U	21
V	22
W	23
X	24
Y	25
Z	26

Class 6S is divided into 8 groups.
Children work out which group they are in using the special code on the left.

You need
a calculator

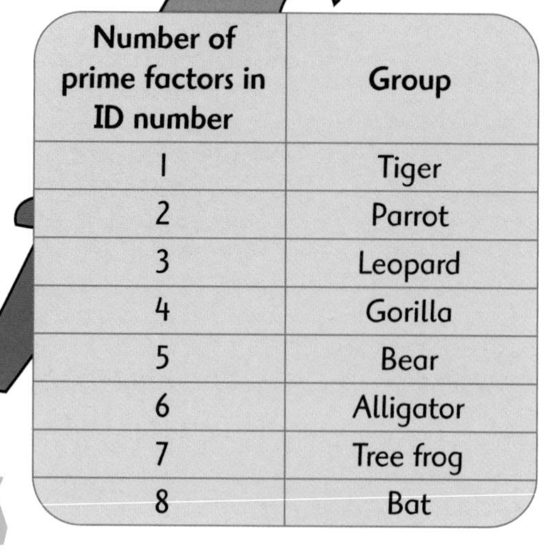

Number of prime factors in ID number	Group
1	Tiger
2	Parrot
3	Leopard
4	Gorilla
5	Bear
6	Alligator
7	Tree frog
8	Bat

1 Use the special code to work out which group you would be in.

- Find the code value of each of your initials.
  The total is your **ID number**.

> Tabitha Green's initials are TG.
> Her ID number is 20 + 7 = 27.

- Find the prime factors of your ID number.

> The prime factors of 27 are $3 \times 3 \times 3$.

- Count the **number of prime factors** in your ID number, then look up the **group** in the table.

> Tabitha's ID has 3 prime factors.
> She is in Leopard group.

2a Use the same method to find out which group these children are in:
- Rhys Hand
- Georgia Foot
- Samuel Brook

b What is special about ID numbers that put children in Tiger group?

3 Here is a different way to put children into groups.
- Add the code value of every letter in their name to find their new ID number.
- Count the number of prime factors to find the group, as before.

a Use this new method to find out which group these children are in now:
- Tabitha Green
- Rhys Hand
- Georgia Foot
- Samuel Brook

b Work out which group you would be in using the new method.

4a Find the smallest possible ID number for each of these groups:
- Bear
- Alligator
- Tree frog
- Bat

b Make up names for children who could be in each of these 4 groups.

1 It is Ben's birthday. His mum has sent into school some different-sized slabs of flapjack for the children to share out equally.
Work out the area of flapjack each child in each group will get.

Group name	Total area of flapjack in cm^2	Number of children in group
Blue	126	3
Yellow	152	4
Red	185	5
Orange	258	6
Green	266	7

2 Use the digits 4, 5, 6 and 7 to complete each multiplication.

You need
digit cards 0–9

a ☐☐☐ x ☐ = 2628

b ☐☐☐ x ☐ = 3948

c ☐☐☐ x ☐ = 3370

d ☐☐☐ x ☐ = 4470

Use digit cards 4, 5, 6 and 7 to help you.

3 Each balloon stands for a single-digit number.
Find the missing number to complete each division.

a 52·96 ÷ 🎈 = 13·24

b 333·6 ÷ 🎈 = 41·7

c 178·2 ÷ 🎈 = 29·7

d 187·5 ÷ 🎈 = 37·5

4 Pick 4 digit cards from a 0–9 set.
Arrange them to make multiplications with two 2-digit numbers.
Find which arrangement gives the largest answer.

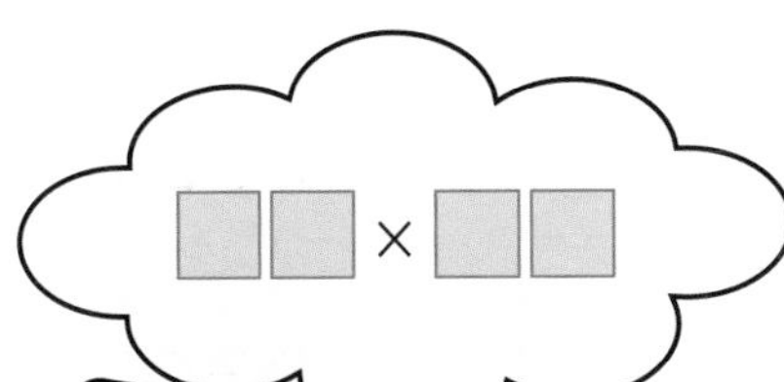

1 Nell works at a park. She has 38 pieces of fencing, each 1 m long, to surround a rectangular nature area.

You need
CM 44

Remember that if the perimeter of the nature area is 38 m, the sum of the 2 sides will be 19 m.

a Complete the table on CM 44 to show all the possible side measurements for the nature area in whole metres.

b Calculate the area of each rectangle.

c Which rectangle has the largest area?

d Which rectangle has the smallest area?

e Write about any patterns you can see in the table. Explain why you think they happen.

2 Nell has 40 pieces of fencing, each 1 m long, to surround a rectangular mini-golf course.
These are some possible measurements for the course:

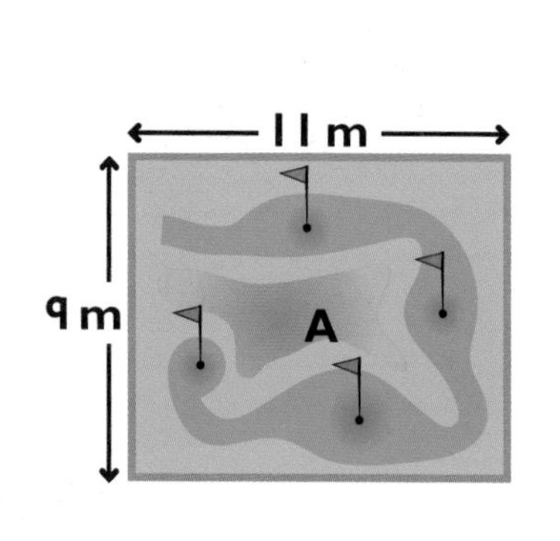

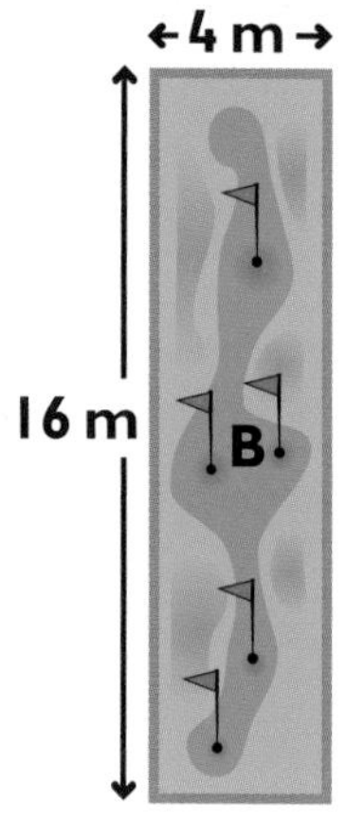

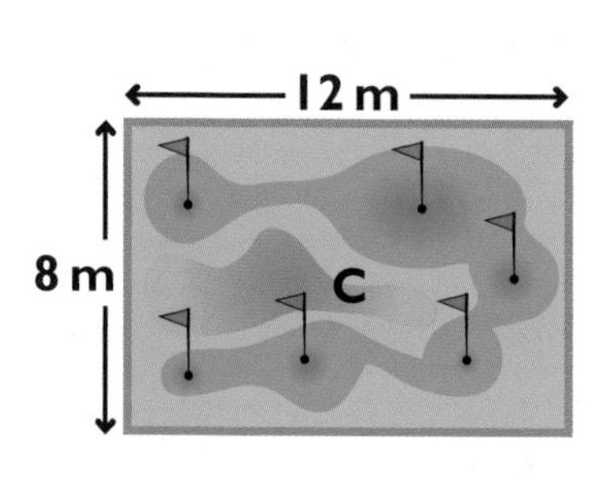

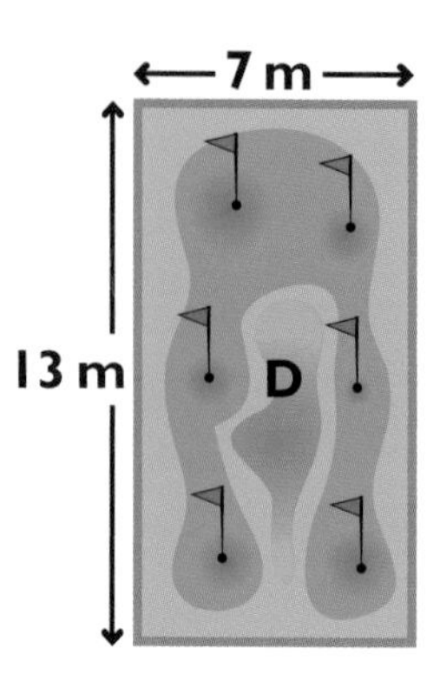

a Which gives the largest area?

b Which gives the smallest area?

c Use CM 44 to list all the possible measurements for the mini-golf course in whole metres.

d Find which measurements give the largest area.

3 Nell has another 42 pieces of 1 m fencing to build a pets' corner.

a How can she use them to make a rectangular enclosure:
- with the largest possible area?
- with the smallest possible area?

b Repeat part **a** for 44 pieces of 1 m fencing.

1a Copy and complete these calculations.

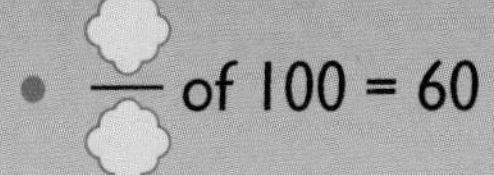

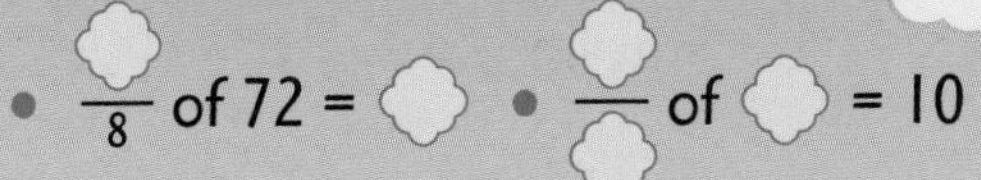

Use number cards to help you.

You need
1–20 number cards

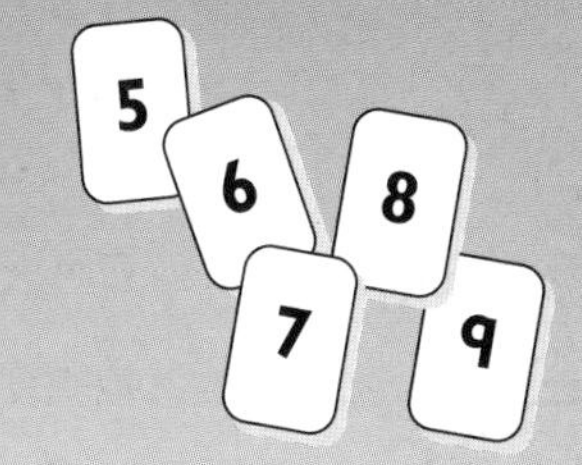

b Find different ways to complete each calculation.
Do not use the number 1 this time.

2a Play **Fraction Roll** with a partner, or in a group of 3.
Take turns to:

- Roll both dice, and use the scores to make a proper fraction.
- Roll again and use the scores to make a 2-digit number.
- Use your fraction and 2-digit number to write a missing-number calculation, with the 2-digit number as the answer.
- Use a calculator to find the missing number.
- Round the missing number to the nearest whole number.
- This is your score for the turn.

The winner is the first to reach 500.

You need
a 1–6 dice
a 0–9 dice
a calculator

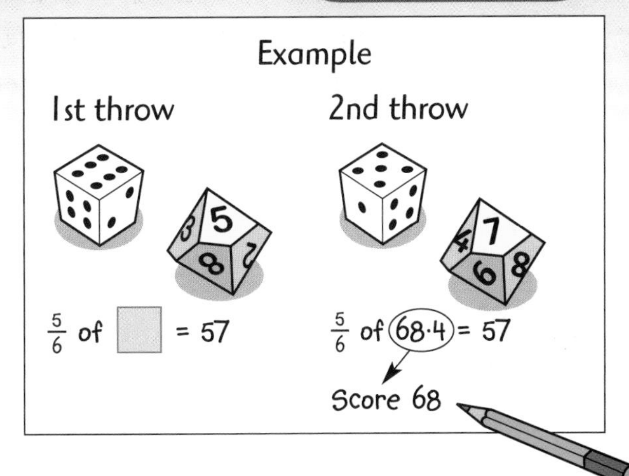

b Play again. This time you may make an improper fraction if you like.

3 Simon and Becky played **Fraction Roll** a different way.
Without using a calculator, they estimated the missing number to the nearest 5.
Then they checked each other's answers with a calculator.
They scored:

- the full amount of the estimate if it was correct to the nearest 5
- half of the estimate if it was correct to the nearest 10
- nothing if the estimate was not correct to the nearest 10.

Try this yourself!

1a Alice cancelled $\frac{600}{2000}$ like this: $\frac{600}{2000} = \frac{300}{1000} = \frac{30}{100} = \frac{3}{10}$

Talk to your partner about how she did it.
How could she have cancelled in one step?

b Here are some more of Alice's examples:

$\frac{25}{75} = \frac{5}{15} = \frac{1}{3}$ $\frac{75}{90} = \frac{15}{18} = \frac{5}{6}$ $\frac{60}{100} = \frac{6}{10} = \frac{3}{5}$

Write how she cancelled each one.
How could she have cancelled in one step?

2 Sylvester investigates the set of proper fractions with the denominator 9.
He finds out which fractions can be cancelled.

$\frac{1}{9}$ $\frac{2}{9}$ $\frac{\not{3}^{1}}{\not{9}_{3}}$ $\frac{4}{9}$ $\frac{5}{9}$ $\frac{\not{6}^{2}}{\not{9}_{3}}$ $\frac{7}{9}$ $\frac{8}{9}$

a Investigate the sets of proper fractions with denominators 10, 11, 12...

b Which sets have no fractions that can be cancelled?

c What can you say about their denominators?

3a Use a calculator to change each fraction to a decimal fraction.

You need
a calculator
the calculator on a computer

$\frac{2568}{3424}$ $\frac{14399}{16456}$ $\frac{3402}{5670}$

b Cancel each of the fractions until it is in its simplest form.

c How can you cancel in one step?

4a Use a calculator to find $\frac{1}{11}$ as a recurring decimal.
Do the same for $\frac{2}{11}, \frac{3}{11}, \frac{4}{11}, \frac{5}{11}$.
How many digits are in the repeating pattern each time?

Try using the calculator on a computer to answer this question. (You can see more digits!)

b Repeat part **a** for $\frac{1}{7}, \frac{2}{7}, \frac{3}{7}$ ... Do these have a repeating pattern?

5 Using the calculator on a computer, investigate patterns of repeating digits for $\frac{1}{13}, \frac{2}{13}, \frac{3}{13}$ ...

1 Fibonacci was a mathematician born in Pisa at the end of the 12th century.
He solved a problem about rabbits by creating this famous sequence.

You can find out more from books or from the Internet.

You need
CM 45
a calculator
scissors
A4 paper
a ruler

1 1 2 3 5 8 13 21 34 55

a What is the rule for finding the next term in the sequence?

b Fill in the next 3 terms on the top line of the table on CM 45.

c Use a calculator to divide each Fibonacci number by the one before it.
Write your answers on the second line of the table.

Give your answers to 3 decimal places.

2 In Fibonacci's sequence the ratio of one number to the one before it gets closer and closer to 1 : 1·618.
This is called the **golden ratio**.
A rectangle with side lengths in the golden ratio is thought to be a very pleasing shape.
It is often used by artists and architects.

a Draw and cut out some rectangles with side lengths that are 2 next-door numbers from Fibonacci's sequence.
Use cm or mm to measure the sides.

b Fold and cut out some rectangles by halving A4 paper again and again.
The side lengths of these rectangles will be in the 'A' ratio, 1 : 1·414 (see page 112).

c Mix up the 2 types of rectangle and swap sets with your partner.
Try to sort them into the 2 ratios, then swap back.
Check your partner's sorting.

1 You are going to create a spiral using Fibonacci numbers.
The 'golden' rectangle on CM 46 has side lengths that are the next-door Fibonacci numbers 144 and 233.

You need
CM 46
a ruler and compasses

- Divide the rectangle into a square 144 mm by 144 mm at one end and a rectangle 144 mm by 89 mm at the other.
  Use the markings to help you.
- Use the previous Fibonacci number to divide that rectangle into a square and a rectangle.
- Continue like this as far as you can.

1
1
2
3
5
8
13
21
34
55
89
144
233

Now use a pair of compasses to draw a spiral.

- Draw a quarter-circle in each square. Start with the biggest square. Set your compasses to the same width as a side of the square you are drawing in.

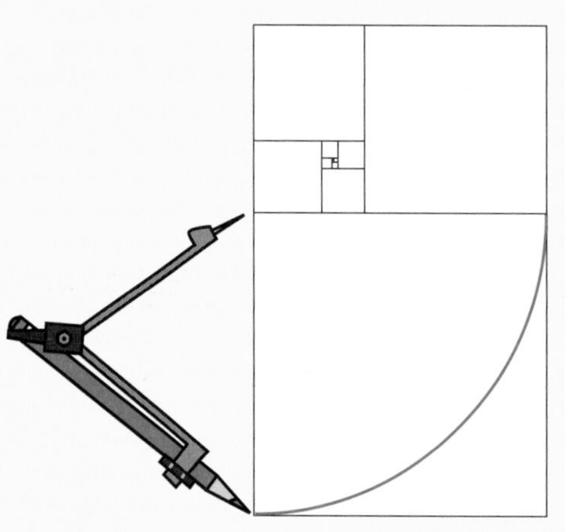

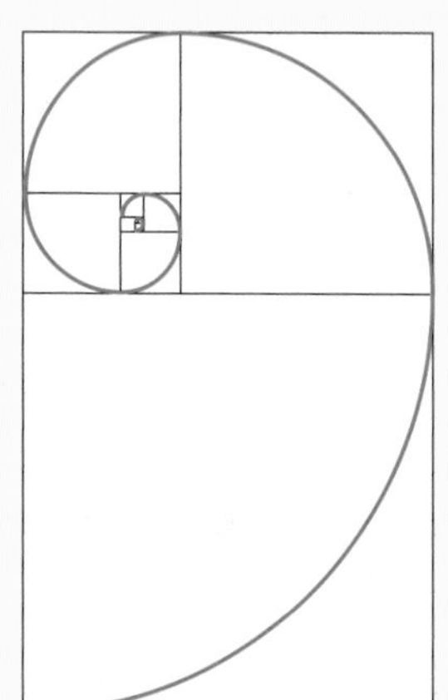

It should look like this when you have finished.

2a Cut out a picture from a newspaper or magazine. Frame it with strips of paper so its side lengths are in the golden ratio.

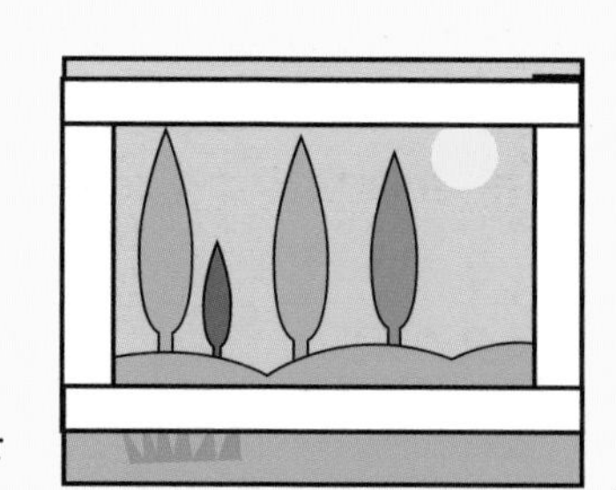

You need
newspaper or magazine
strips of paper or card
scissors

b Now frame it with strips of paper to make an 'A' ratio in the same way.

c Which frame do you think works better?

Look back to page 112 if you are unsure about the 'A' ratio.

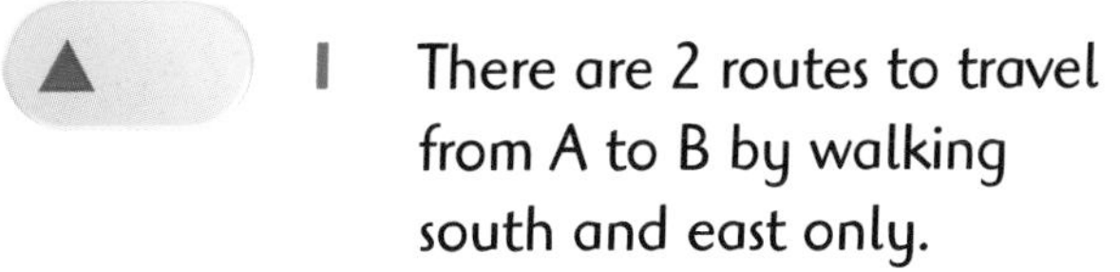

You need
CM 47

1 There are 2 routes to travel from A to B by walking south and east only.

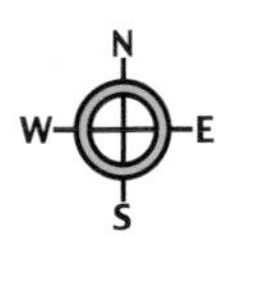

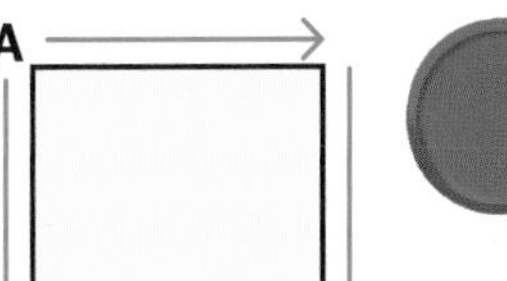

Lindsey gets off the bus at the bus stop. She walks south and east to the Judo Club.

- Find as many different routes as you can for Lindsey to take, walking south and east only.
- Record each route on a different 2×2 grid on CM 47.

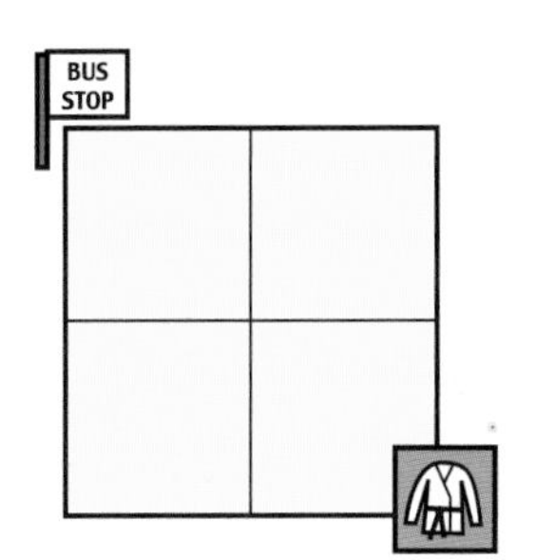

2 Lena gets off a train at the station.

- Find how many different routes she can take from the station to the Judo Club, walking south and east only.
- Use a different 3×3 grid on CM 47 to record each route.

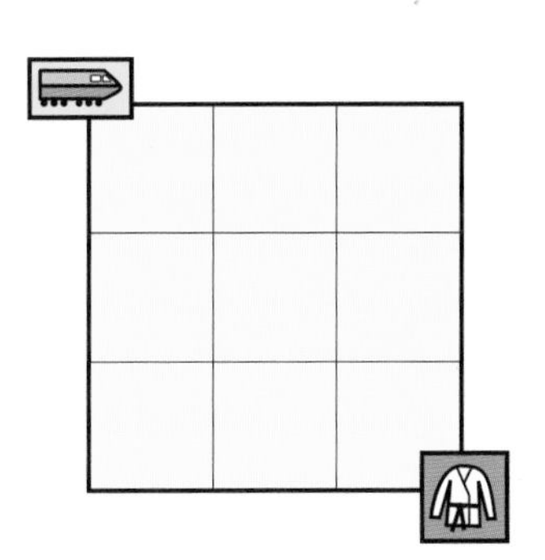

3a Draw a large 3×3 square grid.
Moving down and right only, find out how many routes there are to reach each intersection of the grid.

b Look for a pattern and explain how it works.

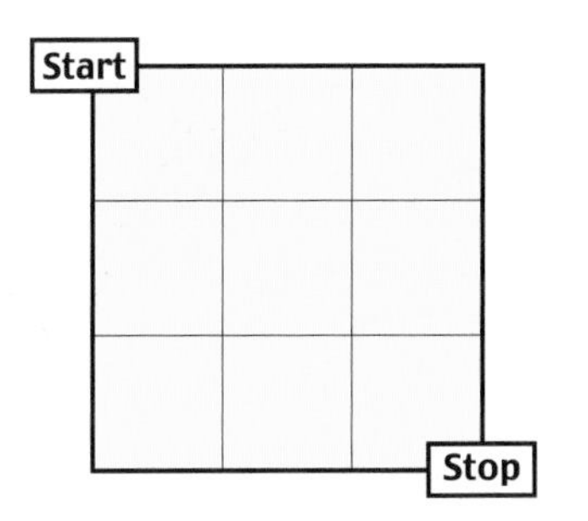

4 Liam walks from the station to the Sports Club.
Investigate the shortest routes he can take.
Explain your answer.

You need
CM 48
CM 49
a ruler
a protractor

1 This bicycle wheel has 3 green spokes.
If you join the ends of the spokes they make an equilateral triangle.

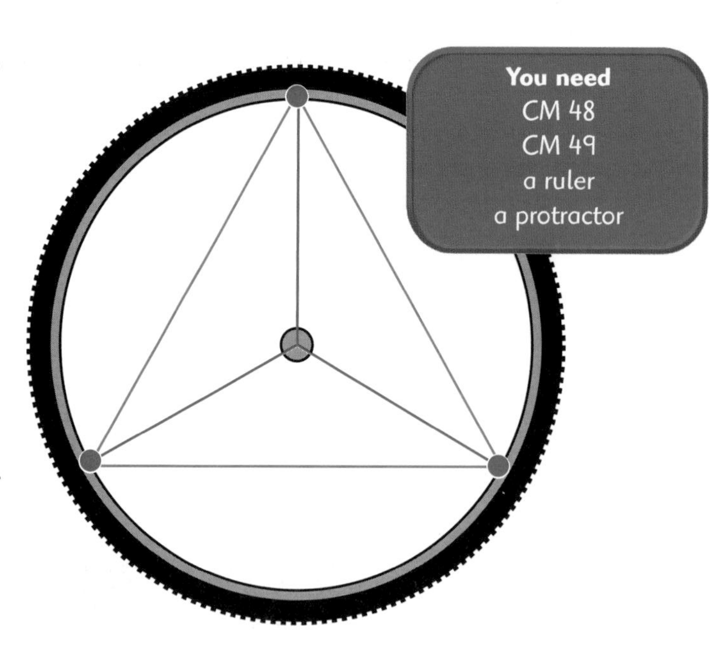

a Measure the angles at the centre of the wheel.

b Measure the angles of the equilateral triangle.

c Write about what you notice.

2a Draw spokes on the wheels on CM 48 and CM 49.
Join the ends of the spokes.
Explore the angles at the centre of the wheels, and the angles you made by joining the ends of the spokes.

b Describe the angles and shapes you make.

3 Use the circles at the bottom of CM 49.

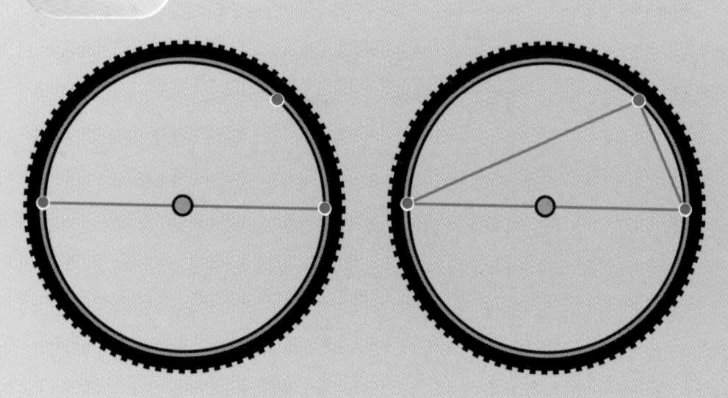

- Draw a diameter line.
- Draw a dot anywhere on the circumference.
- Join the ends of the diameter line to the dot to make a triangle.
- Measure the angles of the triangle.

Explore the angles of other triangles made in the same way.

▲■● **1** An orienteering course has been set up in a park.
Plot the checkpoints on the grid on CM 50.

▲

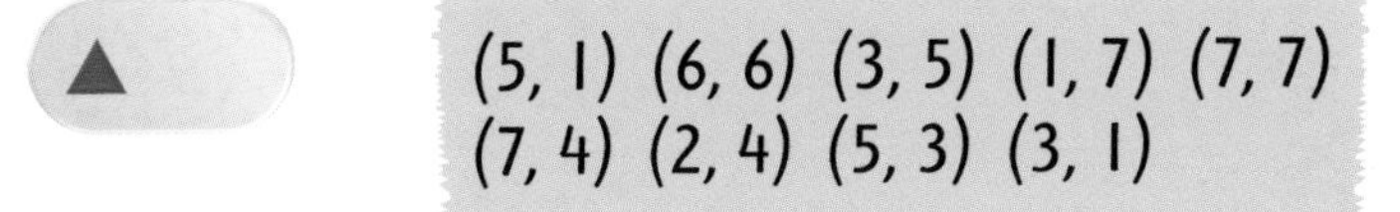
(5, 1) (6, 6) (3, 5) (1, 7) (7, 7)
(7, 4) (2, 4) (5, 3) (3, 1)

■

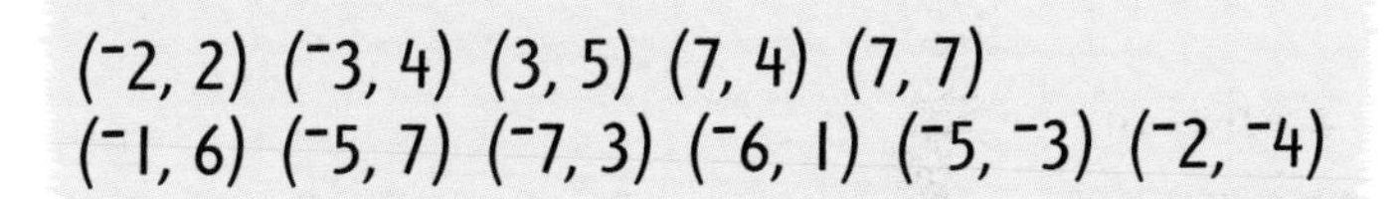
(−2, 2) (−3, 4) (3, 5) (7, 4) (7, 7)
(−1, 6) (−5, 7) (−7, 3) (−6, 1) (−5, −3) (−2, −4)

●

(5, 1) (7, −2) (6, −5) (3, −2) (1, −6) (−2, −4) (−5, −3)
(−6, −7) (−7, −1) (−4, 1) (2, 2) (3, 5) (−3, 4) (−3, −2)

▲■● **2** Find the code letter for each of your checkpoints.
Write them in order to find your secret code word.

Code Grid

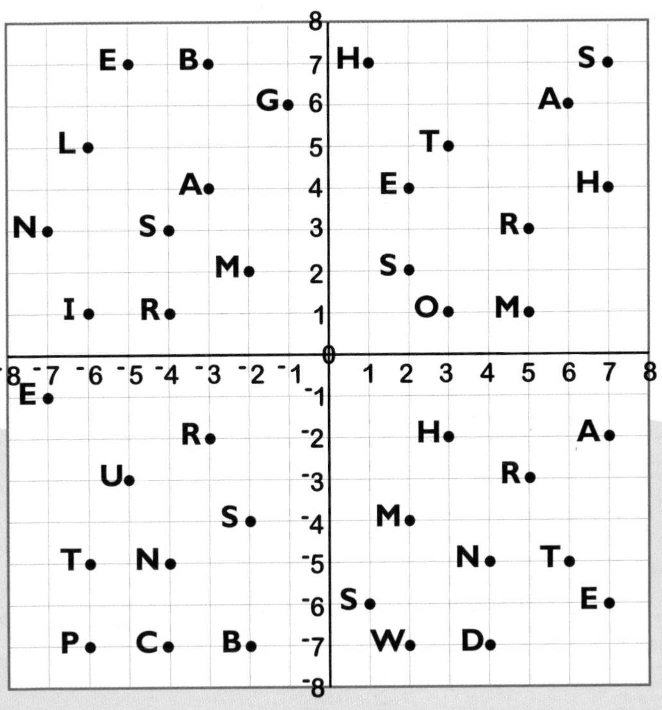

■● **3a** The course starts and finishes at (0, 0).
Join your checkpoints in order, starting and finishing at (0, 0).

b Find the length of the course.
The scale of the map on CM 50 is 1 cm : 0·1 km.

1 In Criss-Cross City there is a roundabout at every crossroads.

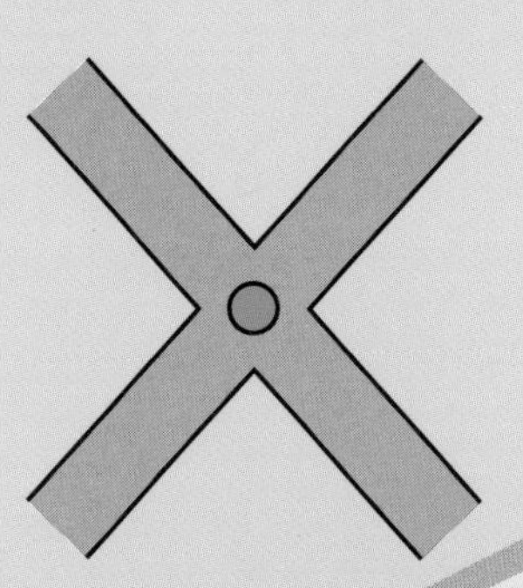

2 intersecting roads
1 roundabout

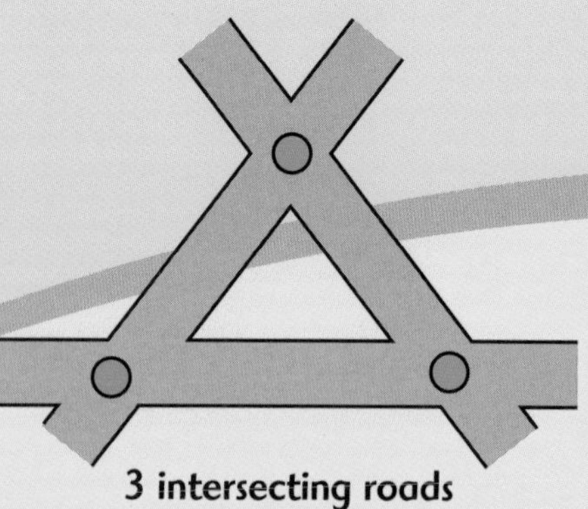

3 intersecting roads
3 roundabouts

Find the maximum number of roundabouts for 2, 3, 4 and 5 intersecting roads.
Record your answers in a table.

Number of intersecting roads	2	3	4	5
Number of roundabouts				

2 Criss-Cross City has plans for 10 intersecting roads.
Look for a pattern in your table from question 1 and extend it to 10 intersecting roads.
Predict the maximum number of roundabouts the City Council will need to install.

3 The Roads Department marks a white line down the centre of each road.

- The line stops when there is a roundabout. A new line starts the other side.
- For example, if there are 3 intersecting roads, there are 9 white lines.

Find the total number of white lines:

a for 4 intersecting roads
b for 10 intersecting roads
c for any number of intersecting roads.

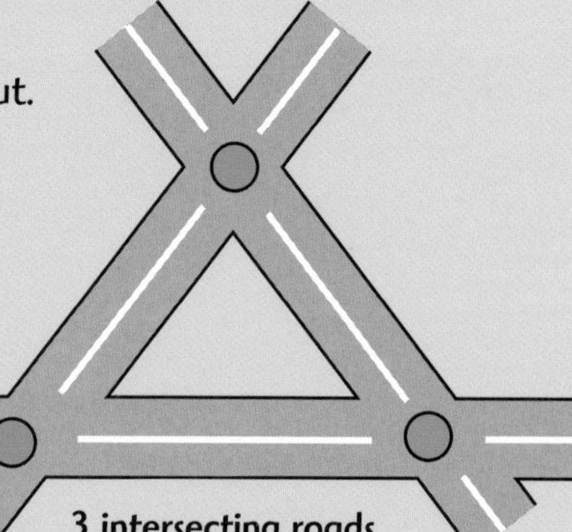

3 intersecting roads
9 white lines